T0316516

Cambridge Elements ☰

Elements in Race, Ethnicity, and Politics
edited by
Megan Ming Francis
University of Washington

(MIS)INFORMED: WHAT AMERICANS KNOW ABOUT SOCIAL GROUPS AND WHY IT MATTERS FOR POLITICS

Marisa Abrajano
University of California San Diego

Nazita Lajevardi
Michigan State University

CAMBRIDGE
UNIVERSITY PRESS

CAMBRIDGE
UNIVERSITY PRESS

University Printing House, Cambridge CB2 8BS, United Kingdom

One Liberty Plaza, 20th Floor, New York, NY 10006, USA

477 Williamstown Road, Port Melbourne, VIC 3207, Australia

314–321, 3rd Floor, Plot 3, Splendor Forum, Jasola District Centre, New Delhi – 110025, India

79 Anson Road, #06–04/06, Singapore 079906

Cambridge University Press is part of the University of Cambridge.

It furthers the University's mission by disseminating knowledge in the pursuit of education, learning, and research at the highest international levels of excellence.

www.cambridge.org
Information on this title: www.cambridge.org/9781108794817
DOI: 10.1017/9781108882224

© Marisa Abrajano and Nazita Lajevardi 2021

First published 2021

A catalogue record for this publication is available from the British Library.

ISBN 978-1-108-79481-7 Paperback
ISSN 2633-0423 (Online)
ISSN 2633-0415 (Print)

Additional resources for this publication at www.cambridge.org/misinformed

(Mis)Informed: What Americans Know About Social Groups and Why it Matters for Politics

Elements in Race, Ethnicity, and Politics

DOI: 10.1017/9781108882224
First published online: May 2021

Marisa Abrajano
University of California San Diego
Nazita Lajevardi
Michigan State University
Author for correspondence: Marisa Abrajano, mabrajano@ucsd.edu

Abstract: This Element examines just how much the public knows about some of America's most stigmatized social groups, who comprise 40.3% of the population, and evaluates whether misinformation matters for shaping policy attitudes and candidate support. The authors design and field an original survey containing large national samples of Black, Latino, Asian, Muslim, and White Americans, and include measures of misinformation designed to assess the amount of factual information that individuals possess about these groups. They find that Republicans, Whites, the most racially resentful, and consumers of conservative news outlets are the most likely to be misinformed about socially marginalized groups. Their analysis also indicates that misinformation predicts hostile policy support on racialized issues; it is also positively correlated with support for Trump. They then conducted three studies aimed at correcting misinformation. Their research speaks to the prospects of a well-functioning democracy, and its ramifications on the most marginalized.

Keywords: misinformation, race/ethnicity, political knowledge, vote choice, public opinion

ISBNs: 9781108794817 (PB), 9781108882224 (OC)
ISSNs: 2633-0423 (online), 2633-0415 (print)

Contents

1 The Politics of Racialized Misinformation   1

2 What Does the Public Know about Socially
  Marginalized Groups?   18

3 The Political Consequences of Racialized Misinformation   35

4 Implications of a (Mis)Informed Public   49

  Bibliography   67

  A further Online Appendix can be accessed at
  www.cambridge.org/misinformed

1 The Politics of Racialized Misinformation

1.1 Introduction

Does an informed citizenry matter for meaningful political participation? In any well-functioning democracy, it is undisputed that citizens should see and hear a wide range of topics and ideas, formulate their political preferences through access to unimpaired alternative sources of information (Berelson et al., 1954; Dahl, 1971, 1989; Delli Carpini and Keeter, 1996; Fearon, 1999; Mutz, 2002; Schumpeter, 1950), and not live in echo chambers (Sunstein, 2018). Access to a broad array of information arguably creates an informed public that, in turn, makes well-reasoned political decisions that reflect and are in line with their preferences.

Nonetheless, this utopian image of an informed citizenry is a far cry from the reality of American democracy today (Campbell et al., 1960). As Bartels (1996, p. 194) aptly and bluntly stated over two decades ago, "The political ignorance of the American voter is one of the best-documented features of contemporary politics, but the political significance of this political ignorance is far from clear." While some scholars have resisted this characterization of voters and instead have argued that voters are minimally informed enough (e.g., Key, 1966; Popkin and Popkin, 1994), another robust body of scholarship has argued that Americans know very little about politics (e.g., Bartels, 1996; Delli Carpini and Keeter, 1996; Hochschild and Einstein, 2015*a*; Lupia, 2016). This latter line of work finds that discussions of democratic competence have drawn a distinction between those citizens who are *misinformed* as opposed to those who are *uninformed* (e.g., Kuklinski et al., 2000; Schaffner and Roche, 2016). According to Kuklinski et al. (2000), the uninformed can be defined as individuals holding no beliefs about the correct answer to a factual question, whereas those who are misinformed hold a false or unsubstantiated belief about the correct response. As Flynn, Nyhan and Reifler (2017) note, "while scholars have long lamented public ignorance about politics, misperceptions (i.e., being misinformed) may be an even greater concern. In particular, misperceptions can distort people's opinions about some of the most consequential issues in politics, science, and medicine."[1]

This state of affairs is somewhat discouraging, especially when one takes into account that Americans are increasingly turning to unmediated news sources unconstrained by journalistic norms, such as online blogs, or posts on social media platforms that are not susceptible to traditional forms of journalistic

---

[1] For examples, see scholarship by Scheufele and Krause (2019), Hochschild and Einstein (2015*a*), and Hochschild and Einstein (2015*b*)

norms (Lajevardi et al., 2020). Reliance on these information sources increases the likelihood of exposure to misinformation or false news stories, which often play to fear through sensationalist coverage that may in turn give rise to moral panics (Anspach and Carlson, 2018). At no time were the political consequences of misinformation so apparent than in the 2016 presidential election when voters regularly reported relying on social media and other forms of unregulated information sources as a principal source of information (Allcott and Gentzkow, 2017; Carlson, 2018). Examples of misinformation in the online sphere during that period are rife, with headlines in 2016 stating "Pope Francis shocks world, endorses Donald Trump for president" and "ISIS leader calls for American Muslim voters to support Hillary Clinton."[2]

In this Element, we focus our attention on misinformation about political and policy facts. Unpacking how and in what ways misinformation matters for politics remains a very pressing issue in the extant scholarship (see, for example, Boussalis and Coan, 2017; Flynn et al., 2017; Grinberg et al., 2019; Hochschild and Einstein, 2015*b*; Lewandowsky et al., 2017; Schaffner and Luks, 2018; Thorson, 2016; Wood and Porter, 2019). For instance, in a study of Twitter users, Grinberg et al. (2019, p. 3) find that partisan leaning was associated with the sharing of content from fake news sources; of those who shared any political content on Twitter during the 2016 election, fewer than 5% of people on the left or in the center ever shared any fake news content, compared to 11 and 21% of people on the right and extreme right, respectively. Similarly, in a study of tweets about the leading presidential candidates during the 2016 election, Barberá (2018) finds that registered Republican users were three times as likely as Democrats to share fake news stories on Twitter.

We depart from the existing research by focusing on misinformation on a specific area of policy facts. Namely, we examine how much misinformation exists in the American public *about socially marginalized groups*, paying special attention to the policies and issues that are directly relevant to them. Thus, we draw a distinction between the types of misinformation currently studied, such as those pertaining to death panels and the Affordable Care Act, the controversy over Obama's religious identity, as well as the more recent "Pizzagate" (e.g., Lopez and Hillygus, 2018; Nyhan, 2010; Schaffner and Luks, 2018). While these forms of misinformation may or may not matter for electoral behavior, they omit a large form of misinformation that likely is linked to political and social behavior: misinformation about stigmatized socialized groups.

---

[2] www.cnbc.com/2016/12/30/read-all-about-it-the-biggest-fake-news-stories-of-2016.html

We consider a social group as "a collective of persons differentiated from others by cultural forms, practices, special needs or capacities, structure of power, or privilege" (Young, 1990). What makes a collection of people into a group, according to Young (1990) is "less some set of attributes its members share than the relation in which they stand to others." The social groups that we focus on have historically been excluded from the polity, and such exclusion, in fact, continues to persist to this present day. Specifically, we focus our attention on the major ethnic/racial groups in the United States namely, Asian Americans, Black Americans, Latinos, and White Americans, as well as Muslim Americans. Our research includes Muslim Americans for several reasons. While the marker "Muslim" is of course an ascriptive religious identifier, the group is an increasingly stigmatized and racialized minoritized group (see, for example, Jamal, 2009; Oskooii et al., 2019; Said, 1978; Sediqe, 2020; Selod, 2015; Sides and Gross, 2013). Their racialization stems from their stereotypical depictions and communication to the public as anti-American, foreign, misogynistic, and violent (Said, 1978). The attacks on September 11, 2001 saw Muslim Americans increasingly linked to terrorism (Calfano et al., 2017). And, research has shown that in the 2016 presidential election, anti-Muslim attitudes were the most important predictor of Trump support aside from party identification (Lajevardi and Abrajano, 2019), further highlighting the group's centrality and low political positioning. Coupled with their racialized and marginalized status, such groups are especially vulnerable to misinformation in light of the way they are portrayed in an overwhelmingly stereotypical manner by the mass media.

Why study this particular domain, you may ask? We offer several reasons that, we believe, are particularly compelling to help advance our understanding of the role of information in politics. First, socially marginalized groups constitute a politically, socially, and economically vulnerable segment of the United States. Currently, these groups constitute an increasingly significant share of the nation's populace at roughly 40.3%. Latinos comprise the largest share at 18.3% of the population, followed by Black Americans at 13.4%, Asian Americans at 5.9%, and multiracial Americans at 2.7%. Muslim Americans comprise about 1.1% of the population (Lajevardi, 2020).[3] In a mere 25 years, Census demographers predict these groups will together surpass White Americans to become the majority of Americans. Latinos will increase to 24.6% of the US population, Black Americans remaining approximately the same at 13.1%, Asian Americans 7.9% and multiracial Americans will be 3.8% of the US population. The U.S. Muslim population is projected to grow to be the second largest

---

[3] www.pewresearch.org/fact-tank/2018/01/03/new-estimates-show-u-s-muslim-population-continues-to-grow/

religious group in the country by 2050.[4] The fact that the share of Americans from socially marginalized groups represent such a considerable share of the current and future population, makes it, in our minds, even more critical to know how much Americans actually know about these groups of individuals, especially as it relates to the issues and policies that are most pressing and relevant to them.

Second, and on a related point, the vast majority of the most current and controversial policies that have risen to the forefront of American politics are now highly racialized in nature. What we mean by this is that the frames and discussions surrounding these policies, such as immigration, criminal justice policies, climate change, welfare, affirmation action, terrorism, and national security, as well as health care, are often couched in some sort of explicit racial language, particularly as it relates to the target group/recipient of these policies (Abrajano and Hajnal, 2015; Gilens, 1996; Pérez, 2016; Tesler and Sears, 2010). As a case in point, the American public is largely unaware that most immigrants in the United States are here legally.[5] A 2018 Pew study found that while 75% of immigrants in the United States are here legally, only 45% of Americans know this. What's more, only 33% of Latinos knew this fact, and only 43% of Blacks. As we will discuss in great detail in Section 2, not only do our own results corroborate these findings, but they also demonstrate that the public is, by and large, highly misinformed about socially marginalized groups.

Third, because of the way the media portrays socially marginalized groups, and the few opportunities that we have to negate and challenge them, we expect their portrayals to be especially vulnerable to misinformation, given the preponderance of stereotypes, tropes, and falsehoods that surround socially marginalized groups. An abundance of research has documented that when these socially marginalized groups are portrayed by the mass media, they are frequently done so by employing stereotypes and tropes. And such a phenomenon is true not only in the news media but also in the entertainment industry (for Latinos and immigrants, see Chavez (2001, 2013); for Black Americans, see Hunt (1999, 2005)). As a result, these depictions have a largely negative impact on how the public evaluates these various social groups and the public policies associated with them (for Muslim Americans, see Lajevardi (2020); for Black Americans, see Gilens (2001); for Latinos, see Pérez (2015)). Given that such opinions and preferences are largely built upon stereotypes as opposed to fact-based information about each of these groups, there is reason to

---

[4] www.cnn.com/2018/01/10/politics/muslim-population-growth-second-religious-group-trnd/index.html

[5] www.people-press.org/2018/06/28/shifting-public-views-on-legal-immigration-into-the-u-s/

believe that the public is largely misinformed about a significantly large portion of the population.

To date, the existing scholarship has largely overlooked how misinformation matters for policies that target the country's most vulnerable and marginalized populations. Understanding how misinformation about social groups factors into one's political decisions and behaviors, particularly as it pertains to vote choice, also remains an open question. While journalists have written extensively on the public's high levels of misinformation about social groups, the political consequences of this misinformation remain largely ignored in the scholarly literature. This omission, we contend, is a significant oversight, especially since misinformation can be very difficult to correct and may have lasting effects even after it is discredited (Nyhan and Reifler, 2015). One potential consequence is that marginalized groups could be targeted and silenced ahead of future elections, further muting their political power.[6]

In this Element, we seek to answer the following two questions: who among the US public is most likely to be misinformed about socially marginalized groups, and is being misinformed about these groups politically consequential? We contend that the degree of misinformation among the general public about social groups is high. Yet we also argue that the degree of misinformation is not uniform, and varies across the public in meaningful and important ways. Our theory and argument focus on several main factors that, we believe, most strongly predict misinformation: partisanship, racial predispositions, social group membership, and news source. We further assert that misinformation carries important political consequences – namely it shapes how individuals decide who to vote for and whether they support or oppose a range of policies.

Why would misinformation be linked to these two types of political behaviors? Once again, we turn to the existing scholarship for guidance. First, we know that socially marginalized groups in the United States are overwhelmingly portrayed negatively by the mass media, with an over-reliance on stereotypes and tropes (for Latinos and immigrants, see Chavez (2001, 2013); for Black Americans, see Hunt (1999, 2005); for Muslim Americans, see Shaheen (2003); for Asians, see Larson (2006)).

Based on the existing research, we also know that one's existing predispositions, particularly those pertaining to the social group in question can also heavily influence opinions of that group (Jardina and Traguott, 2019). There is no doubt that these predispositions are shaped by what individuals watch

---

[6] www.buzzfeednews.com/article/craigsilverman/extremists-disproportionally-target-and-silence-latinos

on the news and in the mass media, along with what they read in newspapers, social media, and other outlets. Yet, at the same time, we think it is imperative to consider the predictive effects of these factors independently from one another. That being the case, we consider the role that racial attitudes play in explaining levels of misinformation. Namely, we expect individuals with more racial animus to be more misinformed about social groups. Additionally, social group membership as well as political ideology could potentially play a role in explaining levels of misinformation. Specifically, we contend that those who identify as politically conservative, whether it be expressed through their political ideology or partisanship, to be more misinformed about social groups. Informed by Jardina and Traguott (2019), we expect White Americans to report higher levels of misinformation, vis-à-vis Black Americans, Latinos, Asian Americans, and Muslim Americans.

We test our research questions by leveraging both observational and experimental methods and techniques. First, to gain a baseline understanding of what the American public knows about socially marginalized groups, we designed and fielded an original survey ($N = \sim 4{,}000$) that included fourteen different fact- and policy-based questions that pertain to these groups.[7] These questions form the basis for our "misinformation" measure, which serves as the foundation for our subsequent analyses. Moreover, the survey asked respondents for their policy opinions on issues that directly impact socially marginalized groups. Such issues include immigration, affirmative action, terrorism/Muslim ban, and crime. Our survey also included a variety of individual-level measures such as demographics, political leanings, and other attitudinal attributes pertaining to social groups (e.g., racial resentment).

To determine the causal relationship between misinformation and political behavior, we designed three experimental studies, all of which were conducted using online surveys. Both Study 1 ($N = \sim 800$) and Study 3 involved the use of a convenience sample fielded through Amazon Mechanical Turk (combined $N = \sim 1900$). Our second study had the largest sample of about 4,000 respondents, and was embedded in our original survey instrument described previously. For consistency sake, the experimental design was similar for all three studies. Respondents were randomly assigned to either a treatment or control group, where the treatment groups received a factual statement about one of three specific policy issues (welfare, the environment, crime), and where

---

[7] We partnered with Lucid to conduct this survey, which uses a nationally weighted convenience sample. Altogether, our survey includes approximately 1,000 survey respondents from each of the five social groups – Asian Americans, Latinos, Muslim Americans, and Whites.

the control group, in contrast, received no such information. The experimental studies were designed to test whether exposing subjects to correct information would lead to a reduction in hostile policy support. We expect the treatment effects to be more pronounced amongst the misinformed, since they are the ones who should be most likely to update their incorrectly held beliefs when provided with factual evidence to the contrary. Ultimately, our comprehensive research design seeks to draw on both observational and experimental survey techniques to systematically gauge the degree of misinformation about socially stigmatized groups in the American public as well as to address the issue of causality.

1.2 Regulated News Sources and Portrayals of Social Groups

Where do most Americans get their information about socially marginalized groups? Undoubtedly, a large segment of the populace relies on the mass media for most of their information about these groups. The high rates of residential segregation along the lines of ethnicity or race in the United States means that most individuals do not actually come into personal contact with those outside their own social group on a regular basis (Reardon et al., 2015). Thus, it stands to reason that the media plays a critical role in exposing the public to information about these groups.

Recognizing the prominent role that the mass media plays in our society, scholars have devoted a great deal of time and attention to studying it. The research has demonstrated the mass media's ability to shape a whole range of political outcomes – but perhaps, most importantly for our research, the media can exert influence on one's political attitudes and opinions (Druckman, 2004; Druckman and Nelson, 2003). The power of the media to affect how we think about virtually all aspects of our daily lives, from current events and politics to the latest film and television, means that we rely heavily on the media as a valuable source of information. And today, accessing this information is not only easier than ever, but is also readily available twenty-four hours a day, seven days a week.

In theory, widespread access to readily available information should be viewed favorably in a representative democracy. But in practice, numerous concerns and unintended consequences have emerged. Most notably, the surge of misinformation or "fake news" are some of the challenges facing this new media environment (Berinsky, 2015; Nyhan and Reifler, 2010). Yet at the same time, bias in the media has long persisted and has been particularly problematic in the portrayal and depiction of socially marginalized groups such as Black Americans, Latinos, Asian Americans, and Muslim Americans, often relying on stereotypes or tropes (Berg, 1990; Dalisay and Tan, 2009; Fujioka, 1999; Hunt and Ramon, 2010; Larson, 2006; Tyree, 2011). And in the aftermath of 9/11, stereotypes of Muslim Americans have worsened and their portrayals have witnessed a sharp increase in the mass media (Kozlovic, 2007; Lajevardi, 2021; Shaheen, 2007).

Countless studies have documented this bias. Take, for instance, the fact that news outlets disproportionately cover violent crimes at rates much higher than their actual occurrence in society. These "crime news" stories also focus on non-whites (e.g. Black Americans and Latinos) as the perpetrators, far more often than they do whites (Gilens, 1996; Giliam and Iyengar, 2000). Such news portrayals also depict Black Americans using stereotypes such as being violent and overly demanding on the government (Gilens, 1996). More recent work links crime with immigration, particularly immigrants from Latin America (Chavez, 2008; Farris and Mohamed, 2018).

A study conducted by Larson (2006) seeks to determine whether this bias extends to all major media, including television, film, newspapers, radio, and magazines. Specifically, she systematically analyzes the representation of the four largest minority groups in the United States: Black Americans, Native Americans, Latinos, and Asian Americans. She compares entertainment media with news media, and pays special attention to the coverage of social movements for racial justice and politicians of color. Her findings reveal that, regardless of the minority group represented, the media frames racial/ethnic minorities in remarkably the same way – first, the focus is on exclusion, followed by stereotyping that distinguishes between "good" racial/ethnic minorities and "bad" ones. Finally, a story that justifies racial inequality in American society is presented. One of the reasons for the persistence of these scripts/frames, Larson (2006) contends, stems from the fact that the mass media is overwhelmingly dominated by White Americans at all levels – from the journalists and producers to high-powered executives.

Latinos have been most frequently depicted through the lens of immigration, with images that are primarily negative, derogatory, and dehumanizing in nature – pests, cockroaches, invaders, wetbacks, etc. (Berg, 2002; Chavez, 2008; Santa Ana, 2002). A study by the National Association of Hispanic Journalists (NAHJ) reports that crime and immigration are the two main issues that are associated with Latinos. The tone of such stories is also far more negative than positive. Moreover, Abrajano and Hajnal (2015) find that immigration news coverage is largely negative, largely focused on Latinos, and largely focused on the negative policy issues associated with immigration. Such patterns in the content and frames used in immigration news articles therefore contribute to the predominance of the "immigrant threat" narrative. Pérez

(2016) reaches a similar conclusion, and finds that immigration news coverage tends focus much more undocumented versus legal immigrants.

Tyree's (2011) study of African American portrayals on television offers a similar conclusion. She analyzes ten reality television shows airing in 2005 and 2008 to investigate whether producers cast participants who fit into traditional and new African American stereotypes. Her analysis reveals that all ten shows had at least one participant who fit into stereotypical characters, such as the "angry black woman, hoochie, hood rat, homo thug, sambo, and coon." Likewise, Hunt and Ramon (2010) document the limited opportunities for Black actors in the entertainment industry, often constrained to stereotypical roles of Black Americans living in the "ghetto." And even in news reports of missing children, Min and Feaster (2010) finds that the news media vastly under reports the number of missing Black children, in comparison to official statistics of missing white children.

Stereotypes and tropes also dominate the media portrayals of Asian Americans. These include references and depictions of Asian Americans as the model minority (Dalisay and Tan, 2009; Fong, 1998), the perpetual foreigner, the "yellow" peril, and references to American Orientalism (Kim and Chung, 2005). The model minority stereotype, in particular, valorizes Asian Americans as hardworking, intelligent, obedient and law-abiding and has been particularly harmful, given that it typically pits Asian Americans vis-à-vis other racial ethnic minorities. Dalisay and Tan's (2009) study, for instance, found that experimental subjects exposed to TV-mediated messages reinforcing the Asian American "model minority" stereotype were more likely to positively evaluate Asian Americans and to negatively evaluate Blacks than were subjects in either the control group or those exposed to a stereotype countering the "model minority" myth. Moreover, while research to date on Asian American depictions in the mass media has found that their inclusion in television and film is rare (Greenberg, Mastro and Brand, 2002; Larson, 2006), when they are depicted, their national origins are often untraceable and their characters often exhibit "unfavorable stereotypes," such as the inscrutable and dangerous foreigner (Hamamoto, 1994).

Prior to 9/11, Muslim Americans were not considered a salient or visible social group. Until 9/11, many US Muslims – and especially those from the Middle East – had historically and formally been treated as "white" under the law and given the privileges of "whiteness". This was a rare feat, given that many groups that are immediately racialized upon their arrival to the United States. The aftermath of 9/11 and subsequent events have led to a massive shift in attitudes toward Muslim Americans and accordingly, media coverage of Muslim Americans as well. As the frequency of negative Muslim portrayals increased (Lajevardi, 2020), these attitudes became commonplace. Along with Lajevardi's (2020) work, Nacos and Torres-Reyna's (2007) study of the news media's coverage of Muslim Americans examines the three largest New York daily newspapers, and finds variations in the volume of front-page coverage on Muslims during the twelve months before and six months after 9/11. While Muslims rarely made the front pages in the year before 9/11, they appeared with far greater frequency in the months following 9/11.

Ultimately, the problem with these depictions is that the frames used in the media can change the group imagery associated with an issue. By focusing over and over on a specific group, subsequent news coverage can result in evaluations of an issue that are based on attitudes toward the group in question rather than on the issue at hand (Gilens, 1996; Pérez, 2016). The negative associations or stereotypes that are typically used in depictions of socially marginalized groups can result in public opposition toward policies that are associated with a given group (Giliam and Iyengar, 2000). Take for example the issue of welfare; the media's disproportionate coverage of Black Americans in such news stories has led to reduced public support for welfare (Gilens, 1996). The same can be said about increased public negative opinion toward Latinos and support for more restrictive immigration policies (Pérez, 2016; Valentino et al., 2013*b*). In fact, most of the American public believes that the majority of immigrants lack legal status, despite evidence to the contrary (Enos, 2014). As all these studies have shown, it is clear that the media can shape public opinion. Yet if most of the media coverage of socially marginalized groups is biased, then the information that individuals have about these groups will, in turn, likely be full of inaccuracies.

1.3 Unregulated News Sources and Misinformation

Talking to our friends, family members, co-workers, and acquaintances about important matters and current events via social media, in-person, on the phone, or even through text messages are all examples of unregulated information sources. These unstructured and informal conversations are a valuable and rich source of information for many individuals (Huckfeldt and Sprague, 1987; Klofstad, 2010). In this context, conversation can be defined as "the kind of speech that happens informally, symmetrically, and for the purposes of establishing and maintaining social ties" (Thornbury and Slade, 2006, p. 25). Individuals, as a result of these interactions, arrive at meaning through conversation (Pask, 1976). The proliferation and ease of information sharing, especially via social media, means that information is readily and constantly available, yet confirming its accuracy becomes the challenge.

Research by Carlson (2019) and Anspach and Carlson (2018) offers a cautionary tale about about the amount of accuracy that exists in these unregulated media sources. Unlike regulated news sources, where the overwhelming majority undergo a thorough and extensive vetting process, there are no such mechanisms on social media platforms such as Facebook, Reddit or Twitter. In essence, individuals can post and share whatever information they want, regardless of its validity or accuracy. Anspach and Carlson (2018) find that individuals who rely on social media commentary are more prone to be misinformed than those individuals who actually rely on the full news article or a preview of the news article. Similarly, in an experimental study conducted by Carlson (2019), she finds that subjects' rates of political learning differed by media source. Subjects who were exposed to news articles demonstrated far greater gains in political learning relative to subjects exposed to social information. Rather interestingly, her study also reveals that when the participants were provided with information from a like-minded and knowledgeable individual, their levels of learning matched those subjects who only received information from the media.

Another concern that arises from these conversations is the potential to further spread misinformation about marginalized social groups. Recent work by Carlson et al. (2020) finds that political discussion networks are ethnically and racially homogeneous – that is, those we talk to about important matters and events are individuals who are predominantly from the same ethnic/racial background. Because residential patterns in the United States are also heavily segregated along the lines of race/ethnicity (Reardon et al., 2015), there are few opportunities for social groups to interact with one another in their everyday lives. In turn, we have witnessed an alarming trend in the resegregation of K-12 public schools (Orfield and Yunn, 1999),[8] which only exacerbates this problem. A study conducted by the Civil Rights Project at UCLA and the Center for Education and Civil Rights at the Pennsylvania State University finds that the average white student attends a K-12 public school where 69.3% of the school's population is White, 8.1% Black American, 13.1% Latino, and 4.2% Asian.[9] In stark contrast, the typical Latino student attends a K-12 public school where 55% are co-ethnics (Latinos), 11.3% Black American, 25.2% White, and 4.9% Asian

---

[8] https://civilrightsproject.ucla.edu/research/k-12-education/integration-and-diversity/resegregation-in-american-schools/orfiled-resegregation-in-american-schools-1999.pdf

[9] www.civilrightsproject.ucla.edu/research/k-12-education/integration-and-diversity/harming-our-common-future-americas-segregated-schools-65-years-after-brown/Brown-65-050919v4-final.pdf

American.[10] In fact, White Americans attend public schools that are the most racially isolated, while Black American and Latino students are far more likely to be enrolled in public schools where 90–100% of the population is non-white.

Taken altogether, opportunities for individuals from stigmatized social groups to interact with non-stigmatized group members, and therefore dispel any misinformation that they may have, are likely to be few and far between. The limited instances that we have to talk with individuals from social groups outside our own are especially troubling given the importance of group contact and interaction in reducing prejudice between marginalized social groups and the dominant social group (Allport, 1954). In this seminal work, Allport (1954) adopts a social psychology approach to explaining one of the most effective avenues at decreasing racial discrimination is for white to reside with and work side-by-side with Black Americans and other racial/ethnic minorities. It is these personal interactions that foster deeper connections and understandings, thereby changing one's cognitive schema and altering previously held racial stereotypes and misconceptions. The fact that the current American landscape makes it more and more of a challenge to be in places and spaces that are racially/ethnically diverse makes such an approach increasingly difficult.

1.4 The Power of Directionally Motivated Reasoning

The previous section indicates that what Americans learn about socially marginalized groups from the mass media is, by and large, negative. And for all the reasons discussed, most Americans are limited in their opportunities to challenge the tropes and stereotypes they see in the news or on television programs since they are unlikely to regularly interact with groups outside their own social group. That being the case, much of what the public knows about socially marginalized groups, and in particular the policies associated with them, is largely rooted in what they are exposed to in the media, and thus has the potential to guide their attitudes and perceptions about them (Chavez, 2008; Gilens, 1996; Hunt, 1999; Pérez, 2016).

As Flynn et al. (2017) and others have argued, we posit that individuals engage in directionally motivated reasoning or confirmation bias (Redlawsk, 2002; Taber and Lodge, 2006), so that they seek out information that reinforces their existing predispositions. The existing research finds two primary sources that underlie directionally motivated reasoning, via their partisanship and

---

[10] Ibid.

through their existing issue preferences and opinions (Taber and Lodge, 2006). Additionally, and of particular import for our study, is the role of identity threat as an important source of directionally motivated reasoning (Green, 2002).

1.4.1 Social Identity

If White Americans' identity is being threatened by questions about the changing demographics and increased diversity of the United States, then social group membership could very well help explain misinformation about social groups. Hochschild and Einstein (2015*b*, p. 587) offer a nuanced explanation of the important relationship between misinformation and group membership:

> For the active misinformed, political activity and knowledge of incorrect facts become mutually reinforcing through the mechanism of group membership. The concordance with like-minded others between beliefs and actions, even if the beliefs are mistaken, renders attitudes far more stable. Thus the active misinformed are remarkably difficult to edge toward the Jeffersonian ideal of informed activity. Persuasion is usually a waste of time; what may be required is conversion.

The salience of group membership, then, may mean that any attempts to correct misinformation of stigmatized social groups will be difficult, especially if its misinformation about out groups.

Earlier, we provided a definition of how we conceptualized and imagined a social group. Yet we wish to be clear that defining a particular population as a social group does not imply that all group members are the same, share the same experiences, or have the same goals or aspirations. Numerous scholars, including Roger Smith (1997, 2003), have shown how citizenship and inclusion in the US polity was defined ascriptively in terms of race, religious, and gender classifications (see also Goldberg, 2002; Ngai, 2014). As these studies indicate, political inclusion and exclusion were the product of explicit public policies, particularly US immigration policies, which were intended to maintain the United States as a White Protestant nation and to materially privilege the white population (Lipsitz, 1998; Lopez, 1997). These ascriptive understandings, in turn, have been found to affect the development of political thought within non-white communities, as well as approaches to and engagement with political and collective action (Cohen, 1999; Dawson, 1995; García Bedolla, 2005, 2015; Gutierrez, 1995; Jones-Correa, 1998; Kim, 1999, 2000; Parker, 2009; Tate, 1994). All of these factors derive from individuals' social position and in turn, inform how the media, elected officials and political elites depict these social groups. Given the positioning of White Americans at the top of the racial hierarchy in the United States, with Latino, Black Americans, Asian Americans and Muslim Americans below them, there is strong reason to believe that White Americans may be more misinformed, relative to the other social groups.

1.4.2 Racial Attitudes

We hypothesize that individuals' preexisting racial attitudes also serve as another important determinant that explains the kinds of information people seek out. A growing body of research confirms the importance of racial attitudes in predicting a multitude of political outcomes – from one's vote choice (Tesler and Sears, 2010), and policy preferences, particularly those that are linked to a social group (Gilens, 1996; Pérez, 2016), to their partisan affiliation (Abrajano and Hajnal, 2015), and evaluations of candidates (Mendelberg, 2001). Racial attitudes also help to explain how individuals evaluate socially stigmatized groups. Both Hochschild and Einstein (2015*a*) and Jardina and Traguott (2019) find that White Americans who hold negative assessments of Blacks are the ones most likely to adopt the birther rumor. Taken altogether, in light of the strong predictive power that racial sentiment can play in explaining nearly every aspect of our political actions and decisions, we also have strong reason to believe that this measure would strongly predict how informed, or misinformed, one is about socially marginalized groups.

However, how to best capture and measure racial attitudes is something that has plagued researchers. The overt manifestation of racial attitudes – or what has come to be known as "old-fashioned racism" – and support for policies further marginalizing nonwhites appeared to diminish (Mendelberg, 2001; Tesler, 2012). By the mid-twentieth century, most Whites expressed a willingness to reject racist arguments that Blacks were intellectually and biologically inferior (Mendelberg, 2001). Publicly espousing beliefs rooted in old-fashioned racism eventually became "taboo," and the once-familiar appeals to white supremacy began to abate (Kinder and Sanders, 1996; Mendelberg, 2001).

The paradox between endorsing racially egalitarian principles while opposing policies that would engender such principles is known by a myriad of terms, including symbolic racism (Kinder and Sears, 1981), modern racism (McConahay, 1986), racial resentment (Kinder and Sanders, 1996), subtle prejudice (Pettigrew, 1997), and aversive racism (Dovidio, 1986). In line with recent studies, we use the racial resentment measure established by Kinder and Sanders (1981) in our analysis.

1.4.3 Partisan and Ideological Affiliation

Based on the previous research (e.g. Ahler and Sood, 2018; Hochschild and Einstein, 2015*a*; Jardina and Traguott, 2019; Lajevardi et al., 2020), we also expect levels of misinformation to vary by one's political leanings (Ahler and Sood, 2018). Jardina and Traguott (2019) find variations along the lines of partisanship, with Republicans being more misinformed than were Democrats and Independents. We therefore hypothesize that Republicans will be more misinformed about social groups than are Democrats and Independents. But along with partisanship, one's political ideology could also certainly be a meaningful predictor of misinformation of social groups. That being the case, those identifying as politically conservative may demonstrate greater levels of misinformation than those who consider themselves to be political moderates or liberals.

It is an undeniable fact that liberal and conservative political coalitions are firmly sorted along the lines of race in the United States (see Mason, 2018; Tesler, 2016). Take the fact that partisan affiliation is highly polarized by race; a mere 14% of the registered Republicans identify as nonwhite, while 43% of Democratic registered voters consider themselves to be non-white. The same divides are also reflected when looking at the ethnoracial composition of Republican versus Democratic elites, particularly in the US Congress. In turn, Republican officials uphold and advocate for policy positions that uphold the preferences of their constituents, primarily conservative White Americans, whereas Democrats push for more progressive policies that are more closely aligned with socially marginalized groups.

Thus, Flynn et al. (2017) purport the notion that "ideology may affect the extent to which people engage in directionally motivated reasoning." Jost, Glaser, Kruglanski, and Sulloway (2003) and others have argued that political conservatism is associated with a tendency toward directionally motivated reasoning due to its association with personality constructs that might influence the relative strength of accuracy goals. For example, political conservatives typically score lower on items assessing openness to experience on personality or values inventories. Instances of backfire effects – where corrections result in a strengthening of political misconceptions – have indeed been observed more frequently among conservatives (e.g. Nyhan and Reifler, 2010; Nyhan et al., 2013). However, the broader set of evidence suggests that directionally motivated reasoning is common among all individuals.

1.4.4 News Source

As we discussed earlier in this section, a persistent, negative bias exists in the way the mass media portrays socially marginalized groups. Another source of bias in the news media pertains to political ideology/partisanship. Today's consumer is no longer restricted to just a handful of news outlets from where they can learn about current events and the latest political happenings. Individuals can now seek out whatever media outlet best suits their tastes, be it from traditional broadcast news, 24/7 cable news, or social media platforms that are carefully curated to align with their preferences. As a result, they can also choose news sources that most closely align to their political preferences and beliefs. Ample studies have documented the political biases in US media outlets (see Budak et al., 2016; DellaVigna and Kaplan, 2007; Min and Feaster, 2010). Perhaps the best example of this bias is Fox News, which has made little secret of promoting an ideologically conservative approach to news making. Breitbart News, which was established more recently in 2007, has quickly garnered a reputation as a far-right media outlet (Farkas and Schou, 2018; Min and Feaster, 2010). MSNBC, on the other hand, is considered to be left-leaning on the political ideological spectrum, and its coverage reflects that perspective (Martin and Yurukoglu, 2017).

If we were to concentrate on the intersection of political and racial biases in media coverage, there is strong reason to believe that conservative media outlets would likely propagate racial stereotypes, especially if we consider the "racialization" of many of the most pressing issues today, such as immigration, crime, welfare, affirmative action, and terrorism (Abrajano and Hajnal, 2015). The end result may very well be even more acute biases in the portrayal of socially marginalized groups in conservative media outlets, relative to more middle of the road or left-leaning media sources (e.g. CNN, *New York Times*, *Washington Post*, MSNBC). A study conducted by Homero et al. (2012) provides suggestive evidence to support this contention. They find a strong and positive relationship between conservative Republicans and their likelihood of watching Fox News which in turn is associated with negative perceptions of Mexican immigrants and greater support for restrictive immigration policies. Also, over a 15 year period between 2001–2016, Lajevardi (2021) finds that FOX's coverage of Muslims and Muslim Americans is more negative than on CNN and MSNBC.

Taken altogether, there is little doubt that bias in the US media has been and continues to be a pressing problem. The plethora of studies documenting the negative portrayals of socially marginalized groups in the mass media indicates that how the mass public thinks about and assesses these groups could very well be influenced by what they watch, read and hear.

1.5 Plan of the Element

In the next section, we introduce our measure of misinformation of socially marginalized groups. We measure misinformation based on fourteen different survey items that tap into individual's *factual knowledge* about socially marginalized groups. To be clear, then, our measure of misinformation is not based on conspiracy theories or political rumors, which has been used by previous researchers of misinformation (e.g. Jardina and Traguott, 2019; Miller et al., 2016; Nyhan and Reifler, 2015). We consider an individual to be misinformed if they answer any of the survey questions incorrectly. Based on all these responses, we then created an aggregate measure of misinformation. The empirical analysis begins by analyzing just how informed the public is about these various social groups. We then compare levels of misinformation by partisanship, social identity, news source, and racial resentment. Section 2 also includes a multivariate analysis to determine which of these factors best predict being misinformed about socially marginalized groups. These models not only control for our key factors of interest, but also a whole range of demographic and political attributes. The section concludes with a discussion of several robustness checks that we conducted to assess the validity of our misinformation measure.

Section 3 examines the political consequences of being misinformed about socially marginalized groups. Namely, we focus on people's policy evaluations as well as their vote preferences. Our survey also included a set of racialized policy questions that directly relate to stigmatized social groups. The policies that we focus on are immigration, affirmative action, criminal justice, welfare, and environmental justice policies. We expect an association between misinformation and policy preferences to exist, so that being misinformed is associated with greater support for a restrictive stance on the issue in question. Finally, there is also strong reason to believe that misinformation about social groups helps to explain voter decision-making for the 2016 and 2020 presidential elections. In particular, we expect the misinformed to lend their support to the Republican presidential candidate, which in the context of these two elections would be Donald Trump.

Our findings reveal that not only are those who are misinformed more likely to support restrictive racialized policies, they were also more likely in 2016 to lend their support to then presidential nominee Trump who ran on numerous platforms targeting stigmatized groups. These results indicate that a misinformed public detrimentally impacts policies targeted at stigmatized social groups in American politics.

A concluding section addresses a fundamental normative question. Is it possible for individuals to reduce their levels of misinformation, and does doing so cause them to alter their political behavior? From a normative standpoint, we would think that if individuals are provided with "correct" information about socially marginalized groups, perhaps their hostility toward them on specific policies pertaining to these groups would be reduced. To address this critical question, we conducted three distinct experimental studies. The experiments allow us to test whether a causal relationship between providing factual information and shaping policy support exists. Nonetheless, the experiments yield null results in the aggregate, though we do discover small effects among specific subsets of the sample, namely among republicans and those with high racial resentment.

This final section also discusses the broader implications of our study and offers a series of next steps and future avenues of research for scholars studying a range of issues, spanning from public opinion and citizen misinformation and competence, to scholars in a variety of areas in American politics. All told, our research provides both important normative and empirical insights on the current state of American politics and the health of our democracy in the United States.

2 What Does the Public Know about Socially Marginalized Groups?

In this section, we focus on the public's levels of misinformation regarding these various social groups. Our analysis begins with a discussion of the survey instrument that we use, followed by some basic descriptive statistics. We then go on to analyze how well the four factors that we identified explain the public's levels of misinformation, even when accounting for a range of demographic attributes, including political ideology, religious affiliation, socioeconomic status, and age.

Here we enumerate our specific hypotheses with regards to the predictors of political misinformation of social groups:

H1: We expect levels of misinformation to vary along the lines of social group membership, political preferences, news source, and racial attitudes.

H1a: Specifically, we hypothesize that White Americans, conservatives/Republicans, those who rely on conservative news outlets, and the most racially resentful to exhibit the greatest amounts of misinformation.

H2: Misinformation about one's own social group should be lower, relative to misinformation of out-groups.

2.1 Measuring Political Misinformation

We spent a great amount of time thinking about the most appropriate way to measure misinformation about the major social groups in the United States. Misinformation can be understood in a myriad of ways. Both Jardina and Traguott (2019) focus on political rumors, whereas others have focused their attention on political conspiracy theories (e.g., Lewandowsky et al., 2017; Nyhan and Reifler, 2010; Swami, 2012).

Importantly, Kuklinski et al. (2000) make a significant distinction between being uninformed (those holding no belief about the correct answer to a factual question) versus being misinformed (holding a false or unsubstantiated belief about the correct response). As Flynn et al. (2017) note:

> While scholars have long lamented public ignorance about politics, misperceptions (i.e., being misinformed) may be an even greater concern. In particular, misperceptions can distort people's opinions about some of the most consequential issues in politics, science, and medicine.[11]

Another way to assess political information, or lack thereof, is to examine the aggregate number of either "don't know" or "no answer" responses provided by each respondent on the political misinformation questions. Yet this measure of nonresponse has been the subject of much debate and discussion by scholars over what these responses are actually comparing.

Our definition of misinformation is in line with Flynn et al.'s (2017) definition of a misperception: "factual beliefs that are false or contradict the best available evidence in the public domain" (p 128). This measure, therefore, does not exclusively focus on conspiracy theories or rumors, unlike previous studies of misinformation (Miller et al., 2016). To be sure, alternative measures of misinformation constitute is an avenue of research that we encourage future scholars to pursue.

The main goal behind developing this measure of political misinformation about social groups lies in a desire to tap into the public's basic and general understanding about social groups, not specific or esoteric information about them. That being the case, and guided by the existing research, we also included several survey items asking respondents about their knowledge about the major trends in demographic patterns in the United States as this has been a widely

---

[11] For examples, see scholarship by Hochschild and Einstein (2015*a*), Hochschild and Einstein (2015*b*), and Scheufele and Krause (2019).

publicized and discussed phenomenon by the news media. Another area where we suspect misinformation to be high pertains to policies where marginalized social groups are the primary group target or beneficiary. Thus, we developed several survey items to assess what the public knows about policies that directly relate to social groups. In addition, given the previous work on the infamous "birther" question (Jardina and Traguott, 2019), we also include it in our survey. Here are the specific survey items that we asked.

1. What is the population size of the undocumented immigrants in the United States? 1) 10.7 million; 2) 20.1 million; 3) 5.5 million; 4) 15 million; 5) 30.2 million; 6) Don't know/No answer.
    Correct answer: 10.7 million
2. Do you think most of the immigrants who are now living in the United States are here legally, or are without legal status? 1) Legally; 2) Without legal status; 3) Half and half; 4) Don't know/No answer
    Correct answer: Legally
3. The US Census Bureau projects that by 2042, ethnic and racial minorities will comprise the majority of the nation's populace. 1) True; 2) False; 3) Don't know/no answer.
    Correct answer: True
4. In the U.S, Black men are six times as likely to be incarcerated as white men and Hispanic/Latino men are more than twice as likely to be incarcerated as non-Hispanic/Latino white men. 1) True; 2) False; 3) Don't know/no answer.
    Correct answer: True
5. Blacks and Latinos are less likely to live in regions with hazardous waste and substandard air quality on average, relative to Whites. 1) True; 2) False; 3) Don't know/no answer.
    Correct answer: False
6. All US universities are legally allowed to consider race in their undergraduate and graduate admission policies (e.g. Affirmative Action). 1) True; 2) False; 3) Don't know/no answer.
    Correct answer: False
7. Most terrorist incidents on US soil have been conducted by Muslims. 1) True; 2) False; 3) Don't know/no answer.
    Correct answer: False
8. To the best of your knowledge, do you think the following statement is accurate or inaccurate? President Barack Obama was born in United States? 1) Accurate; 2) Inaccurate; 3) Don't know/no answer.
    Correct answer: Accurate

9. How many Muslims are in the United States? 1) Between 50,000–500,000; 2) Between 500,00–1 million people; 3) Between 1 million–2 million people; 4) Between 2 million–5 million people; 5) Between 5 million–10 million people; 6) More than 10 million people; 7) Don't know/No answer.

   Correct answer: Between 2 million – 5 million people

10. Which country has the largest number of Muslims? 1) Saudi Arabia; 2) Iran; 3) Pakistan; 4) Indonesia; 5) Afghanistan; 6) Don't know/No answer.

    Correct answer: Indonesia

11. For the following federal programs – food stamps, welfare, social security, and public housing – are the primary recipients Blacks, Whites or about the same? 1) White; 2) Black; 3) About the same; 4) Don't know/No answer.

    Correct answer for food stamps: White

    Correct answer for welfare: White

    Correct answer for social security: White

    Correct answer for public housing: About the same

2.2 Survey Design and Data

We fielded these misinformation survey items using an online convenience survey that was conducted by Lucid.[12] While the survey itself is not a nationally representative sample, for our purposes, what was most critical was to have a large enough sample of each social group. Thus, the sample consisted of 965 Asian American respondents, 976 Black respondents, 944 Latino respondents, and 1,014 White respondents. We also interviewed 833 self-identified U.S. Muslim respondents. Our survey was conducted exclusively in English, due to financial constraints associated with fielding multilingual surveys.

Additional survey items included partisanship, racial resentment, news consumption, and social group identity. We also surveyed respondents on their demographic attributes (sixteen survey items), and news consumption (two survey items). The additional survey items pertaining to demographics asked respondents for the following: religious affiliation, gender, and socioeconomic status (household income and education). To capture one's news consumption, we asked survey respondents what media source they rely on for information

---

[12] We used Lucid Marketplace, which utilizes independent, third-party data partners. According to Lucid, "suppliers are evaluated on the three most important aspects of sample supply – response quality, accepted completes, and consistency." More information can be found here: https://luc.id/quality/

on politics. Table A1 (online) provides summary statistics for all variables employed in the full sample of our study.

2.3 How Misinformed Is the Public?

Before we discuss our aggregate measure of misinformation, we think it is important to present the distributions of each of our knowledge questions. To that end, Figure 1 presents the percentage of individuals who provided a misinformed response to each of the factual questions presented. Here, we note several interesting patterns.

First, respondents faced considerable difficulty in accurately assessing the recipients of public services – social security, food stamps, and welfare. Fully 74% of respondent offered a misinformed answer on the primary recipients of social security. Those who provided a misinformed response either thought that Black Americans are the main recipients, or Black and White Americans equally. We see a similar pattern with respect to food stamps and welfare.

A majority of Americans, 56%, are also misinformed about the legal status of U.S. immigrants. This majority believed that most of the immigrants residing in the United States lack legal status, yet that is not the case. These findings are consistent with previous studies (e.g., Enos, 2014) and public opinion polls that point to the American public's overestimation of the number of undocumented immigrants living in the country. The fact that the media and

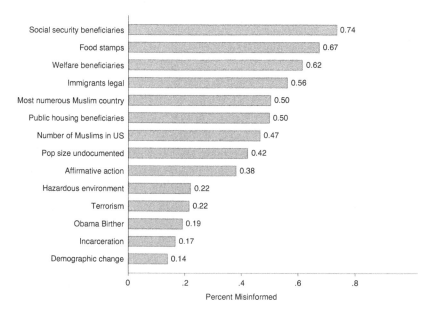

Figure 1 Percent of respondents providing a misinformed response, by question

prominent political elites constantly focus on the need to reduce the "flood" and "wave" of immigrants entering the United States is one likely reason why the public is so prone to being misinformed about the actual size of this particular immigrant population (Chavez, 2001, 2008s).

At the other end of the spectrum, we are also interested in knowing which questions generated the lowest levels of misinformation. We find that respondents are least misinformed about future changes in the racial/ethnic composition of the US population, racial differences in incarceration rates, and Obama's birthplace (the birther question). The percent of misinformed respondents on these facts is 14%, 17%, and 19%, respectively. While the percentage who are misinformed on these questions is significantly less than it is for the questions regarding welfare beneficiaries, it is still rather remarkable that approximately one out of five Americans inaccurately indicate that President Obama was born outside of the United States.

We also observe differences in misinformation levels based on the survey item response options. That is, respondents perform better (e.g. are less misinformed) when they are provided True/False responses versus multiple choice responses. As Figure 1 highlights, notice that the three questions (President Obama's birthplace, incarceration rates, and future demographics of the United States) where respondents report the lowest levels of misinformation are the true/false questions. Yet the top six survey items where respondents reported the highest amounts of misinformation were designed as multiple-choice questions (ranging from three to four response categories). The extent to which respondents are guessing, and therefore have a higher chance of selecting the correct answer when there are only two responses as opposed to three or four, is certainly one possibility. Yet the fact that all but one of our six True/False questions is where respondents report the lowest levels of misinformation, this make us less inclined to conclude that respondents are merely guessing the correct answers.

We now turn to a discussion of our aggregate measure of misinformation. Recall that we created this measure based on an additive scale that includes all of the knowledge questions described previously, with higher values denoting greater levels of misinformation, whereas lower values denote those who are the least misinformed. The misinformation scale ranges from 0–13. We exclude nonresponses from this measure (e.g. don't know or no answer), since we wanted to be certain that our measure is capturing an inaccurate response to these specific survey items, as opposed to survey respondents opting to provide a nonresponse.[13] The average score on the misinformation scale was 5.8

---

[13] Recall that question #11 is actually four separate questions, which brings us to a total of thirteen questions that comprise this aggregate measure of political misinformation.

(with a standard deviation of 2.6), which indicates that the average respondent in the survey was misinformed about nearly half of the knowledge questions. This estimate generally aligns with the existing research recognizing that the American public generally possesses a minimal amount of political information (Delli Carpini and Keeter, 1996; Miller et al., 2016), though our study is somewhat distinct since we are specifically focusing on a certain type of political information – that which pertains to marginalized social groups.[14]

In Figure 2, we present the distribution of this measure, which offers several notable insights about the public's levels of misinformation about social groups. First, few respondents are at the tail ends of the distribution. That is, less than 5% of our respondents are what one could describe as "fully" informed about social groups (meaning that they answered all of the knowledge questions correctly or only answered one question incorrectly). Yet we also observe about 11% of individuals who provided inaccurate answers to *all* or nearly all of the information questions. This suggests that the American public does appear to have *some* knowledge about socially marginalized groups, but it does not seem to be a considerable amount. If we focused on the distribution of respondents who fall above and below the midpoint (5.8), the percentage of respondents who score below the midpoint, thus being less misinformed, is ~42%. The percentage of those who are above the midpoint is ~58%.

2.3.1 Is the Public Equally Misinformed?

As we stated in our first hypothesis (H1), we expect certain pockets of the public are more misinformed than others about social groups. Such variations should be the most pronounced along the lines of social identity, partisanship, news source, and racial resentment. When we compare the misinformation rates across the five social groups, a number of notable patterns emerge (see Figure 2). First, it suggests that White Americans and Asian Americans report higher levels of misinformation than Blacks, Latinos, and Muslim Americans. Note that these differences are statistically significant from one another at conventional levels, which offers us some assurance that the differences in misinformation across these social groups are meaningful. At the same time, we recognize that the magnitude of difference between White and Asian American's average level of misinformation (3.4) is not considerably larger than it is for Blacks (3.2), nor for Muslim American respondents, who

---

[14] Most of the literature on political information uses measure of "textbook" or factual political misinformation, such as the number of members in Congress or identifying the name of the current Supreme Court Justice. There is, however, a vigorous debate on the validity of this measure in capturing political misinformation (see Abrajano (2015) for a brief summary).

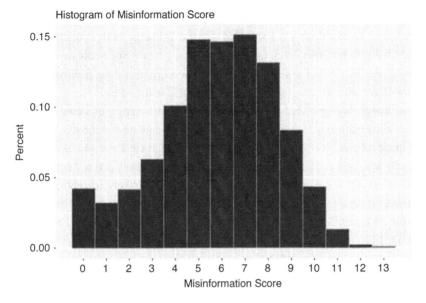

Figure 2 Distribution of aggregate measure of misinformation

report the lowest levels of misinformation. Nonetheless, if we consider this difference on a larger scale, such differences would likely be substantively meaningful.

Next, we examined misinformation levels by partisanship and, consistent with the existing research (Grinberg et al., 2019; Jardina and Traguott, 2019), meaningful differences in levels of misinformation do emerge by one's partisan identification. As we hypothesized, Republicans are significantly more misinformed than are Democrats and Independents (see Figure A2 (online)). Here, the differences are quite substantial, with a 0.7 difference on a 0-13 scale between Republicans and Democrats in their misinformation levels. Likewise, the difference between Republican and Independents' misinformation score is 0.9. What this roughly translates to is Republicans providing one more incorrect question than do Democrats and Independents. Comparatively speaking, the differences across partisanship produce larger differences in misinformation than do the differences across one's social group.

We now examine the average levels of misinformation by the type of news source people rely on. In order to test our main argument that much of what individuals come to learn about social groups stems from what they learn in the news media, and media outlets in general, we asked them to share with us their media consumption habits. Specifically, we asked them the following question: "How much do you rely on the following sources for your information on politics?" The responses ranged from not at all, very little, somewhat, and a great deal. Respondents were provided with the following twelve outlets, which included both traditional news sources along with a range of social media platforms: Radio, CNN, FOX, MSNBC, ABC News, CBS News, Breitbart, *New York Times*, *Washington Post*, Twitter, Facebook, and Reddit.[15]

Although we provided respondents with a wide range of news sources (including cable outlets, social media, and mainstream news sources), for ease of interpretation, we focus on five news sources that are known to have a particular ideological leaning: Fox News Breitbart, MSBNC, *New York Times*, and CNN. Of these sources, respondents were most likely to rely on CNN ($\mu = 2.51$ on a 1–4 Likert scale where higher values indicate greater reliance), followed by FOX ($\mu = 2.30$), *New York Times* ($\mu = 2.20$), and MSNBC ($\mu = 2.17$). They were less likely to rely on Breitbart ($\mu = 1.53$). Our analysis indicates that level of misinformation does vary by news source, so that individuals relying on conservative news outlets, such as FOX and Breitbart, report higher levels of misinformation than those who turn to CNN or MSNBC as their primary source of information. Avid FOX consumers averaged 6.72 on our aggregate misinformation scale, with Breitbart at 6.97. In contrast, CNN and MNSBC viewers averaged 6.26 and 6.36 respectively.[16]

Finally, we explore variations in misinformation based on an individual's level of racial resentment. Jardina and Traguott's (2019) work highlights the importance of racial animus in helping to explain and understand who is susceptible to misinformation and political rumors. Given the role that racial attitudes play in fueling misinformation, we considered it important to understand whether political misinformation vary by one's racial attitudes. For our analysis, we categorize racial resentment into three categories: those with high, medium, and low levels of resentment.[17] Our findings reveal important variations in misinformation of social groups based on one's level of racial resentment. Individuals who are the most racially resentful report the greatest amount of misinformation about social groups, relative to those in the

---

[15] This survey item was based on the one used in the CCES. Each of these variables is coded such that higher values denote a great deal of reliance on the specific information source in question.

[16] *New York Times* readers were slightly more misinformed ($\mu = 6.51$) than CNN and MSNBC viewers, though still less misinformed than FOX consumers.

[17] We develop these three binary variables of misinformation as follows. Those who are grouped "high racial resentment" are among the 75th quartile and above on the racial resentment scale in a specific social group (in a specific survey instrument). Those in the "medium racial resentment" group were ranked between the 25th and 75th percentiles on racial resentment, and those in the "low racial resentment" category are those who scored in the 25th percentile or below on the racial resentment item.

two lower categories.[18] This observation holds even when we look at specific misinformation pertaining to policy, Muslim Americans, and even on specific items, such as the birther question. Similar to Jardina and Traguott's (2019) findings, the patterns we uncover are suggestive of the role that racial resentment plays in understanding how much individuals know about social groups, and as we argue, are shaped to some extent by what they see and learn from the media. They also expand upon the existing research, by highlighting the way racial animus can also determine how misinformed one is about marginalized social groups in the United States.

2.3.2 Are Social Groups Less Misinformed about Their Own Group?

Recall that our second hypotheses (H2) expected misinformation about one's own social group to be lower, relative to misinformation of out-groups. That is, Latinos and Asian Americans should be the least misinformed on the questions pertaining to immigration, relative to Black Americans, Whites, and Muslim Americans. Given that approximately 40% of both the Latino and Asian American population are foreign-born, it is reasonable to think that they would be more attuned to the size of the undocumented immigrant population as well as its composition.

The survey items that we posted on affirmative action and racial inequities in environmental living conditions should also bear differences in misinformation levels. We would therefore expect to see lower levels of misinformation on these issues for Blacks and Latinos than we would for Whites, Asian Americans and Muslim Americans. Note that these differences are statistically significant at $p < 0.05$ level. We compare the rates of misinformation on these specific questions, by social group. Figures 3 and 4 present these distributions.

Overall, the findings provide moderate support for our argument. First, we do see that Black Americans seem to be the least misinformed regarding the racial discrepancies in incarceration rates, relative to the other four social groups.[19] Given that Black Americans are the most disproportionately affected by mass incarceration and the criminal justice system more broadly, it is understandable why they would be aware of the systemic racial inequalities that characterize it.

We also find that the degree of misinformation pertaining to immigration varies across social groups. Asian Americans, the social group with the largest

---

[18] The high resentment group averaged $\mu = 6.33$ on our aggregate misinformation scale, while misinformation among those with medium and low racial resentment fell below this value, averaging 5.70 and 5.48, respectively.

[19] This difference, which is statistically significant at conventional levels, lends support for H2.

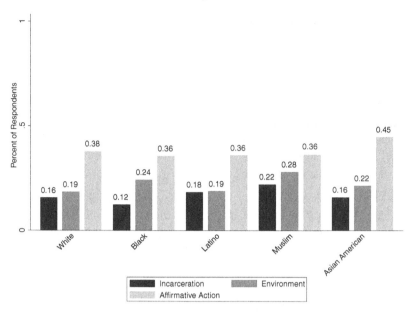

Figure 3 Misinformation levels on incarceration, env't, and affirmative action (0–1), by social group

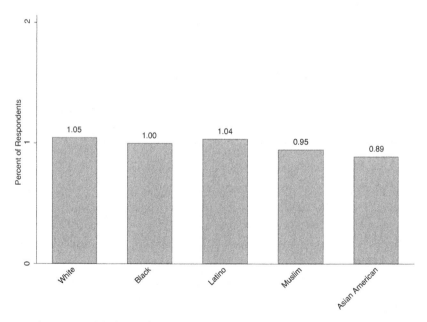

Figure 4 Misinformation levels on immigration, by social group (0–2)

foreign-born population, are the least misinformed about immigration, whereas White Americans report the greatest levels of misinformation. Latinos, the social group with the second largest number of foreign-born individuals, are actually on the higher end of the misinformation scale. In fact, they are quite close to the levels reported by White Americans (1.04 and 1.05 respectively). This finding was rather surprising to us, since we hypothesized that the two largest immigrant groups, Asian Americans and Latinos, would be the least misinformed about factual questions on immigration.

Moreover, on the issue of affirmative action, we see some support for our hypothesis with respect to Black Americans; namely, they are less misinformed on the way affirmative action policies are applied across universities in the United States, relative to Asian Americans. In fact, Asian Americans are the most misinformed social group on this particular policy domain. Perhaps part of the uncertainty on this issue stems from the recent court case on affirmative action, where Asian Americans sued Harvard University for their use of race/ethnicity in their admissions process.[20] We also know that affirmative action is an issue that voters find to be complex; consider that in the pre-election polls pertaining to California's ballot initiative regarding Proposition 16, which would have restored the use of affirmative action in higher education, nearly 43% of Asian American voters were undecided or didn't know about the issue.[21]

Another finding that runs contrary to our expectations pertains to knowledge on the racial inequities in environmental living conditions. For this particular question, we had strong reason to believe that Black Americans and Latinos would be the least misinformed, given that they are the ones who live in these adverse environmental conditions. Yet our findings suggest otherwise. Latinos and White Americans appear to be the least misinformed about the disparate effects of environmental hazards on brown and black communities, when compared to Black Americans, Asian Americans, and Muslim Americans.[22] Although we hypothesized that knowledge would be greater on policies that directly affect one's own social group, we don't find any evidence of that with respect to environmental justice.

Our final test of this hypothesis pertains to misinformation about Muslims and Muslim Americans. Namely, we expected Muslim Americans to be the least misinformed on questions #7, #9, and #10, given that these questions directly impact them in some fashion (see Figure 5, which presents levels of misinformation on Muslim Americans, by social group). What these results

---

[20] www.nytimes.com/2020/02/18/us/affirmative-action-harvard.html
[21] https://aapidata.com/2020-survey/
[22] These differences are statistically significant at $p < .05$ level.

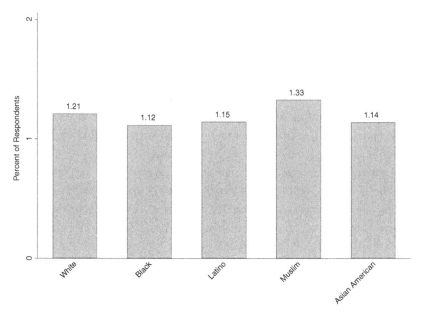

Figure 5 Misinformation levels about muslims, by social group (0–3)

indicate, however, is very minimal support for H2; in fact, these findings actually run contrary to our expectations. Rather, Muslim Americans are the most misinformed about their own group, relative to White, Black, Asian, and Latino participants.[23] This finding is rather surprising, given that we expected groups to have greater levels of knowledge about their own groups, and that mass opinions about Muslim Americans trend more negative than other religious and race groups (except for atheists and at times, Mormons). We also recognize the diversity of the Muslim American population, which perhaps contributes the low levels of awareness about the entire group as a whole.

Overall, these descriptive analyses offer us a more nuanced understanding of the way misinformation varies not only depending on question wording and type, but also by social group, some of whom would have a natural proclivity to seek out accurate information about specific policy domain and areas.

2.3.3 Exploring the Determinants of Political Misinformation

The following analysis estimates a multivariate statistical model to ascertain which of the various factors we explored previously most strongly predicts political misinformation. The model also accounts for other factors that could explain political misinformation, including respondents' socioeconomic and demographic attributes. Figure 6 presents the estimates; in general, the results

---

[23] These differences are statistically significant at $p < 0.05$ level.

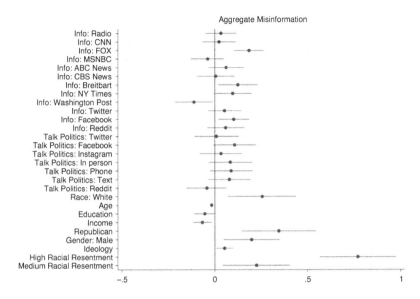

Figure 6 Predictors of aggregate misinformation

support H1 and H1A.[24] Namely, even when we account for a whole host of demographics and political factors, we find that it is White Americans, the most racially resentful, Republicans, and those who regularly rely on conservative news outlets to be the strongest predictors of misinformation. Specifically, the estimates indicate that regularly relying on Fox News and Breitbart is positively correlated with being misinformed about socially marginalized groups.

Taken altogether, these findings provide credence to our hypothesis regarding the predictive power of these four attributes in explains what predicts misinformation of socially marginalized groups. As the existing research has so aptly demonstrated (see Budak et al., 2016; DellaVigna and Kaplan, 2007), clear ideological and political biases exist in the content of news outlets, with Fox News adopting a staunchly ideologically conservative position, relative to other news companies. Breitbart News is also considered to be a far-right news outlet (Farkas and Schou, 2018). Additionally, research by both Lajevardi (2021) and Homero et al. (2012) highlight the predominance of negative coverage of socially marginalized groups in conservative news outlets. Our findings offer further proof of the powerful role that the media plays in shaping our political beliefs and knowledge. In particular, we show how it may be related to shaping the public's views on socially marginalized groups in a negative fashion.

---

[24] Figure 6 corresponds to Table A6 (online).

Our estimates also indicate that men are more likely to be misinformed than women. We find no discernible relationship between political ideology and misinformation about social groups, despite previous research identifying a relationship between political ideology and misinformation. Our findings appear to reflect the argument put forth by Kinder and Kalmoe (2017), who find that the American public is not nearly as ideologically polarized as are political elites. In reality, true ideologues are only few and far between.

Readers may wonder which of the four factors we identified exert the strongest predictive power on being misinformed about socially marginalized groups. To address this question, we calculated the marginal effects for these specific variables of interest, while holding all the remaining variables at their mean or mode. We find that high feelings of racial animus exerts the greatest explanatory power in predicting misinformation about social groups, more so than the other three factors that we focused on. Possessing the greatest levels of racial resentment leads to an average increase of 0.73 on the misinformation scale. That would translate into providing about one more misinformed question on the scale.[25] Amongst those who score in the mid-range of the racial resentment scale, the marginal effect size is significantly lower at 0.19. To put this into context, approximately 27% of the sample are considered to be highly racially resentful, 43% in the middle, and 30% on the low end of the scale.

The marginal effects for our media variable vary based on how dependent individuals are on this news source. That is, individuals frequently relying on Fox News for information is associated with an average increase of 0.52 on the misinformation measure, whereas the effect size for occasional users of Fox News is considerably lower at 0.26. The difference between frequent versus occasional users of Breitbart, however, is less pronounced; regular users are correlated with an average increase on the misinformation scale is 0.29, whereas the effect size is 0.24 for occasional users. It thus seems to be the case that those who turn to Fox News appear to be the most misinformed about socially marginalized groups, relative to those who rely on other conservative news outlets.

The marginal effect of partisanship and those who self-identify as White Americans yield roughly a similarly sized effect on misinformation. Self-identification as Republican is associated with an average increase of 0.32 on the misinformation scale, while the effect size for self-identified Whites is 0.25. Overall, these analyses suggest that individuals' high amounts of racial animus as well as heavy reliance on Fox News as a primary source of knowledge most

---

[25] We calculated the marginal effects for our main variables of interest by setting all the remaining variables are their mean or mode.

strongly predict misinformation about socially marginalized groups. Comparatively speaking, the effects of social group membership (White Americans) and partisanship (Republican) are not nearly as great as the effect of media consumption.

We also believe it is worth investigating whether there are certain characteristics that predict who is the most knowledgeable about socially stigmatized groups. Our analysis suggests that there are far fewer predictors explaining one's knowledge of these groups, relative to the factors predicting one's level of misinformation about them. The estimates from Table A6 (online) indicate that being among the most socioeconomically advantaged and those who rely on *The Washington Post* for political information helps to predict lower levels of misinformation.

While many journalists and political pundits have extolled the influence of social media, the ones we control for, Facebook and Twitter, fail to exert any predictive power on one's misinformation of social groups. Additionally, other attributes that have previously been identified as important predictors of general political misinformation, such as age, have no bearing on our particular measure of misinformation. And while ideology was correlated with misinformation of social groups, partisanship fails to reach statistical significance.

Our models also account for the possibility that who we talk to about politics can influence our awareness of socially marginalized groups. As we discussed in the introduction, the conversations that we have with one another, whether it be through social media or face to face or on the phone, can provide us with valuable information (Carlson et al., 2020; Huckfeldt and Sprague, 1987; Klofstad, 2010). Individuals, as a result of these interactions, arrive at meaning through conversation (Pask, 1976). However, the estimates from our model suggest that political conversations fail to exert any explanatory power on our measure of misinformation.

2.4 Robustness Checks

In this section, we briefly discuss several additional statistical tests to assess the validity of our findings. First, it is entirely possible that some overlap exists in the characteristics amongst those who are the most misinformed – White Americans, Republicans, the most racially resentful, and consumers of conservative news outlets.[26] That is, our analysis assumes that these effects are independent of one another, but it could also be the case that such attributes can have an

---

[26] Only 153 respondents are White, Republican, and have high levels of racial resentment.

additive or interactive effect. To determine whether this is the case, we conducted additional statistical analyses where we created an interaction term that captured those individuals who scored high on the racial resentment scale and also self-identified as White. Moreover, in another set of analyses, we created a variable that captured individuals who self-identified as Republicans and also relied on conservative news outlets. The results from both of these analyses indicate that the interactive terms fail to exert any explanatory power on misinformation about social groups. As such, these factors are appearing to exert an independent relationship with misinformation, rather than an interactive one.[27]

2.5 Conclusion

In this section, we aimed to lay the groundwork for our empirical tests, primarily by way of an original survey that probed a diverse sample of respondents about their knowledge of marginalized social groups in the United States. Specifically, we focus our attention on the four major ethnoracial groups in the United States, as well as Muslim Americans. We conceptualized misinformation in a broad and inclusive manner, taking into account whether individuals are aware of the main policy and issue concerns faced by socially marginalized groups to awareness of the changing demographic characteristics of the nation. By collecting this information, we are able to gain some important insights on just how much knowledge the American public holds about these groups and whether some individuals are more prone to misinformation than are others. Indeed, we find this to be the case. One's levels of racial resentment, partisanship, news source, and social identity help us to understand who is the most misinformed about social groups.

Taking a step back to consider the bigger picture, our results offer some important takeaways and future steps for research. First, it suggests that misinformation about socially marginalized groups is not evenly distributed across the US public. Instead, certain segments within the electorate are more prone to misinformation than others. We find that White Americans, men, the racially resentful, Republicans, and those who turn to Fox and Breitbart for news strongly predict misinformation about social groups. As previous scholars have identified, it is difficult deny the powerful role that racial animus plays in explaining American's political attitudes, beliefs, and behaviors (Jardina and Traguott, 2019; Tesler and Sears, 2010). Our study further contributes to this rich body of work by demonstrating the strong predictive power of racial sentiment on the public's degree of misinformation about he socially marginalized

---

[27] It is also worth noting that the correlation between being White and having high racial resentment is quite low at -0.02 and the correlation between Whites and relying on Fox News is -0.03. The correlation between those who are highly racially resentful and relying on Fox News is 0.12

in the United States. In the next section, we explore the political ramifications of being misinformed.

3 The Political Consequences of Racialized Misinformation

In Section 2, we presented data that shows that the public is largely misinformed about a significant portion of the electorate. We found that misinformation is largely sustained by stereotypes about social groups, rather than fact-based information about them. Along with individual predisposition, misinformation about socially marginalized social groups is also influenced by individuals' reliance on different sources for political information. Partisan sources play an especially vital role in shaping the information gleaned from these outlets to their respective networks. Those particularly vulnerable to this information, moreover, could be developing opinions that are unsubstantiated and biased.

Having established that misinformation about stigmatized social groups is fairly high among the American public, a lingering question remains: Is misinformation about these groups consequential for shaping hostile policy support? In other words, does misinformation about these minority populations matter for the policy attitudes and positions that Americans hold? The sheer volume of misinformation campaigns targeting marginalized populations makes it all the more pressing to understand the racialized policy consequences of being misinformed.

In this section, we perform a series of statistical tests to assess whether misinformation is politically consequential and exerts any predictive power on the policies that individuals support. We pay particular attention to policies across many domains that are racialized, meaning that they target stigmatized groups in the United States (e.g. Enders and Scott, 2019; Gilens, 1996; Michener, 2019; Ojeda et al., 2019).

Theoretically, we expect individuals' policy support to differ based on their levels of political misinformation about social groups. Broadly, we expect that the more misinformed individuals are, the more they will support restrictive racialized policies. Our analyses characterize those who are misinformed as referring to those who hold factually incorrect beliefs about stigmatized social groups. Since misinformation is rooted in stereotypes and is communicated through mediums that are sensationalized, unregulated, and highly partisan, we expect these prejudices to matter for individuals' policy positions.

We also contend that the positive relationship between increased misinformation levels and greater hostile policy support to persist for each of the stigmatized groups we examine. Although misinformation levels differ between groups, we posit that the positive association between being more misinformed and policy support will function similarly no matter a person's membership in a stigmatized social group, given that intergroup prejudice (Eric Oliver and Wong, 2003) and racial resentment (Segura and Valenzuela, 2010), which underlie misinformation, do shape the electoral calculus of non-White voters.

Section 3 dedicates the majority of its attention to presenting results from statistical analyses that explore whether being misinformed explains individuals' support for a whole host of restrictive racialized policies. The section concludes by briefly assessing whether misinformation is politically consequential for the presidential candidates that respondents reported supporting in the 2016 and 2020 presidential elections.

3.1 Measuring Support for Restrictive Racialized Policies

So far, we have shown that political misinformation about groups varies considerably among social groups, among those with varying degrees of racial resentment, and by partisanship. What remains unanswered, however, is whether misinformation about these populations matters for politics. While scholarship has previously examined the empirical link between misinformation and policy support (e.g. Hochschild and Einstein, 2015*b*), this literature has either looked at misinformation more generally, or has looked at public support for non-racialized policies. In this section, we instead ensure that the misinformation and policy support that we examine are both directly related to stigmatized social groups. Here, we use statistical models to establish an empirical link between aggregate political misinformation and a series of policy preferences that directly affect stigmatized groups.

To assess how political misinformation correlates with policy opinions, we asked respondents a battery of questions gauging their policy positions and opinions. Specifically, we focused on several issue areas that directly affect and impact social groups (Abrajano and Hajnal, 2015; Gilens, 1996). These positions centered on crime, affirmative action, environmental risks that affect racial/ethnic minorities, welfare, immigration, and a series of questions relating to Muslims in the United States. While most of these issue areas affect more than one group under consideration, together they capture policy attitudes related to large subsets of Muslim Americans, Asian Americans, Blacks, and Latinos.

Figure 7 depicts mean support for each of the policy issues we asked respondents about in our sample. Respondent answers to these the policy

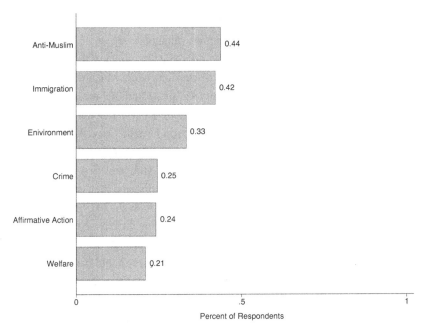

Figure 7 Percent support for restrictive policy position, by issue

questions have been rescaled to range from 0–1, and increasing values indicate more hostile support for the policy. For the purposes of the main analyses, all respondents who refused to provide an answer and selected "prefer not to stay" are dropped from the analysis.

The first policy variable we asked about is an aggregate and additive measure of three immigration policies that ask about immigration generally, as well as about the border wall with Mexico. Immigration, as a policy position, impacts members of many minoritized groups, including but not limited to Asian Americans (Junn and Masuoka, 2008), Latinos (Abrajano and Hajnal, 2015; Valentino et al., 2013b), Muslims (Calfano, 2018; Rippy and Newman, 2006), and even segments of the African American population (Smith, 2014; Waters, Kasinitz and Asad, 2014). We asked individuals to indicate how strongly they agreed with the following statements on a Likert scale ranging from 1–5: (1) "The U.S. Constitution should be changed so that the children of unauthorized immigrants do not automatically get citizenship if born in this country," (2) "The federal government should build a wall on the border of the United States and Mexico," and (3) "Immigration levels to the United States should be decreased."[28] Higher values indicate more support for the restrictive

---

[28] These three items cohere well together, alpha = 0.7632.

immigration policy. Mean support for this aggregate outcome variable is 0.423, with a minimum value of 0 and a maximum value of 1.

The second policy area asks about anti-Muslim policies that are often invoked in the American political discussion over Muslim Americans (Lajevardi, 2020). This variable is composed of an additive measure of support for three distinct policies that are directed toward Muslim Americans. The policies we asked about are related to anti-sharia laws that have been increasingly introduced into state legislatures across the nation (Mitchell and Toner, 2016; Oskooii et al., 2019; Yazdiha, 2014), the "Muslim ban" first proposed by then-presidential candidate Trump in the 2016 election and then enacted in his first year in office (Collingwood et al., 2018; Oskooii et al., 2019), as well as a Muslim registry which was also largely debated during the 2016 election (Aziz, 2017). The questions asked respondents to rate how strongly they agreed with the policy statements on a 1–5 Likert scale: (1) "States should ban sharia law, because unless we pass laws restricting it, sharia law will sweep the nation," (2) "The United States should implement a Muslim registry," and (3) "The Muslim Ban has been effective at keeping our nation safe."[29] Support for these policies is slightly higher than for the aggregate immigration statements, with mean responses measuring 0.439 and answers ranging from 0–1.

Respondents were also asked to indicate their support for affirmative action (Bobo et al., 2000). Public opinion tilts largely against the policy, with a 2019 Pew Research Center study finding that almost three-quarters (73%) of Americans agree that colleges and universities should not consider race or ethnicity when making decisions about student admissions.[30] Affirmative action has long been characterized in the national discourse and in academic settings as a policy that touches a number of racial and ethnic groups – including Asian Americans, Latinos, and Black Americans (Salinas, 2020), gives rise to racial intergroup conflict that pits Asian Americans against Black Americans and Latinos (Gonzalez O'Brien et al., 2020; Kim, 2018), and is rooted in prejudice (Kim, 2018; Moses et al., 2019). Most recently, we saw California voters reject Proposition 16, which would have restored the use of affirmative action policies in the admissions process as well as in hiring. Support for this ballot initiative was particularly mixed in the Asian American community. To assess support for affirmative action, we asked respondents to rank support for the following question on a 1–5 Likert scale which we rescaled to range from 0–1: "Do you think affirmative action programs designed to increase the number of

---

[29] These items also cohere well with one another, alpha = 0.7620.

[30] www.pewresearch.org/fact-tank/2019/02/25/most-americans-say-colleges-should-not-consider-race-or-ethnicity-in-admissions/

underrepresented minorities, such as African Americans, Latinos, and Asians, on college campuses are a good thing or a bad thing?" Mean support for this restrictive affirmative action policy hovered at 0.242.

Our survey also measured support for policies designed to provide environmental protections to racial and ethnic minorities. Scholarship has shown that racial and ethnic minorities are disproportionately proximate to environmental hazards which yield adverse health effects (e.g., Chakraborty et al., 2011), but that swaths of Americans – including whites and nonwhites alike – underestimate the environmental concerns of non-white and low-income Americans and misperceive them as being lower than those of their white and more affluent counterparts (Pearson et al., 2018). Research has also found that racial attitudes have spilled over into attitudes about climate change (Benegal, 2018). In this vein, we asked respondents for their support for the following policy: "The U.S. government needs to take action to reduce the environmental risks that disproportionately affect racial/ethnic minorities." Responses to the statement were also recoded from the original 1–5 point Likert scale to range from 0–1, and mean support for the policy was 0.335.

We measured respondent support for two restrictive policies that are rather well-cemented in the American imagination: crime (Bobo and Johnson, 2004; Peffley and Hurwitz, 2002) and welfare (Gilens, 1996, 2009; Wetts and Willer, 2018). Crime, as a policy issue, had undoubtedly become synonymous with racial and ethnic minorities in the American imaginary. Not only are racial and ethnic minorities more likely to have high levels of contact with the carceral state (e.g., Ghandoosh, 2019; Harris et al., 2020; Taylor et al., 2018; Walker et al., 2020; Weaver and Lerman, 2010), public attitudes about criminal policy are often rooted in racial prejudice (Green, Staerkle and Sears, 2006; Hurwitz and Peffley, 2005; Peffley et al., 2017; Wilson, Owens and Davis, 2015). Some of these attitudes may stem from the fact that Black Americans and Latinos have historically been characterized by a "crime news script" in television news (Giliam and Iyengar, 2000; Gilliam Jr. et al., 1996; Jackson, 2019), though other groups like immigrants (Farris and Silber Mohamed, 2018) and Muslims (Lajevardi, 2021) are also susceptible to criminalized, negative, or violent portrayals. The policy question on crime asks respondents to rate their support for one of two approaches to lowering the crime rate in the United States: more money to tackling the social and economic problems that lead to crime through better education and job training (or) more money and effort to deterring crime by improving law enforcement with more prisons, police, and judges. Those who chose "tackle social problems" were coded as 0, while those who chose "more law enforcement" were coded as 1. Mean support for the hostile crime policy is 0.247.

Finally, respondents were asked about another well-known, controversial, and racialized policy on the American domestic agenda: welfare. Critiques of the "welfare state" were first levied in the 1960s–70s in the aftermath of civil rights disturbances, and were overtly espoused by President Ronald Reagan who expressed the white majority's unease with the perceived expansion of the social safety net (Gilliam Jr., 1999). It is during this period when the infamous trope of the "welfare queen" emerged– politicians and social reformers accused poor Black women of bearing children for the sole purpose of obtaining a welfare check (Collins, 2002; Thomas, 1998). When the public is exposed to images of "welfare queens", it reduces their support for welfare programs, increases stereotyping of Blacks, and heightens support for maintaining traditional gender roles (Gilliam Jr., 1999). Scholarship has found that a new implicit racism exists (Bonilla-Silva, 2015), whereby Whites, through their opposition to welfare spending, implicitly target Black Americans and Latinos (Barkan and Cohn, 2005; Cassiman, 2008). In turn, this can maintain a system of minority oppression and supremacy without explicit acknowledgement, especially when it is uprooted by Christian nationalism (Davis, 2019). Bearing this in mind, respondents in our survey were asked, "Do you want to see Congress increase spending on welfare programs, decrease spending, or keep it about the same?" Answers were coded as 1 (decrease spending), 0 (keep it about the same), and 0 (increase spending). Mean support for the hostile welfare policy is 0.211.

3.2 Unpacking the Relationship between Political Misinformation and Policy Preferences

We begin with two simple statistical tests designed to evaluate how being misinformed shapes restrictive policy support. These two tests unpack the bivariate relationship between being misinformed and hostile policy support. We perform two main statistical analyses for each information state and test this relationship: (1) with an aggregate indicator of being politically misinformed, and next (2) with a suite of disaggregated misinformation indicators.

The aggregate analysis we start with evaluates how being generally misinformed predicts restrictive policy support. As we described in Section 2, our aggregate misinformed measure is constructed by coding each of the binary political misinformation items as value 1 if the survey respondent selected an incorrect answer, and value 0 if they selected "don't know" or the correct answer.

Our second test further examines the relationship between misinformation and restrictive policy support, but we now focus on specific political misinformation questions that correspond to the policy issue at hand. In this case, we attribute a value of 1 to those who select the incorrect answer and a value of 0 to those who select the correct answer or "don't know." We have four "misinformed" binary political misinformation indicators on affirmative action, the environment, crime, and welfare, where we attribute a value of 1 to those who select the incorrect answer and a value of 0 to those who select the correct answer or "don't know."[31] However, because some of our misinformation questions are constructed as additive variables, not all will range from 0–1. For instance, our "misinformed" political misinformation question on immigration ranges from 0–2, $\mu = 0.985$, and our "misinformed" Muslim misinformation variable ranges 0–3, $\mu = 1.187$.

In the analyses that follow, we conduct probit regressions for policy attitudes on affirmative action, crime, and welfare (e.g., Models 3, 5, and 6) because the dependent variables take on values of either 0 or 1, while for policy attitudes on immigration, Muslims, and the environment (e.g., Models 1, 2, and 4) we present OLS regressions since the dependent variables are not binary.

Table 1 presents the results from our first test. Here, we explore the bivariate relationship between our aggregate measure of misinformation and support for restrictive racialized policies. Across the board, we find a positive and significant relationship, providing an initial confirmation that being generally misinformed about socially stigmatized groups increases individuals' hostile policy support on a whole host of issue areas. When we include a suite of control variables in Table A7 (online). this positive and significant effect persists. Consistent with the previous analyses, racial resentment and partisanship continue to predict their policy preferences on these range of issues.

While these findings generally support our expectations, it is also important to assess the magnitude of these effects. To that end, we calculated marginal effect estimates to determine the average effect size of misinformation on explaining one's policy positions. It is particularly useful to compare the effect of misinformation vis-à-vis one particular control that consistently exerted strong predictive power in all of our models: racial resentment. Across all of our models, we find that the marginal effect of being misinformed pales in comparison to the marginal effect of being highly racially resentful on policy attitudes. That is, individuals' holding great amount of racial animus are associated with a far larger increase in their support of a more restrictive stance on racialized policies than one's level of misinformation. While the marginal

---

[31] Response means for each of the variables was as follows: legality of affirmative action policies $\mu = 0.382$, likelihood of living in a hazardous environment $\mu = 0.221$, incarceration likelihood of people of color $\mu = 0.167$, and welfare beneficiaries $\mu = 0.616$.

Table 1 Effects of (aggregated) political misinformation on restrictive racialized policy preferences

	(1) Immigration (Agg) Preferences	(2) Muslim (Agg) Preferences	(3) Affirmative Action Preferences	(4) Environment Preferences	(5) Crime Preferences	(6) Welfare Preferences
Aggregate political misinformation	0.0178***	0.0199***	0.0545***	0.00576***	0.0842***	0.0398***
	(0.00158)	(0.00141)	(0.0100)	(0.00174)	(0.00943)	(0.00979)
N	4,732	4,732	3,618	4,732	4,073	4,010
adj. R^2/pseudo R^2	0.026	0.040	0.007	0.002	0.018	0.004

Standard errors in parentheses

+ $p < 0.10$, * $p < 0.05$, ** $p < 0.01$, *** $p < 0.001$

effect of misinformation ranges from 0.01 to 0.10, the marginal effect of racial resentment ranges from 0.16 to 0.21.[32]

Honing in on one particular issue highlights this differential effect to an even greater degree. On the issue of affirmative action, being misinformed leads to an average increase of 0.04 on the likelihood of taking an anti–affirmative action stance. Yet in stark contrast, the marginal effect of being highly racially resentful is six times greater at 0.24. Taken altogether, these findings help us to better understand what role misinformation plays in predicting one's positions on racial policy issues. While it is certainly the case that misinformation factors into an individual's decision to adopt a particular position on a given policy, even when we account for a wide range of factors such as political affiliations and demographics, its predictive power is far more muted, particularly in comparison to the racial resentment measure.

Results from our second test are presented in Table 2. This test disaggregates the misinformation variable into specific indicators that directly correspond to the policy issues being examined. We find the positive and statistically significant relationship between misinformation and hostile policy support persists with two exceptions: (1) we lose statistical significance in Model 3 when we examine the relationship between being misinformed about affirmative action and support for affirmative action policy, and (2) the coefficient's sign flips and becomes negative and significant in Model 4 when we examine the statistical relationship between misinformation about hazardous living environments and support for restrictive environmental policies. Table A8 (online) presents results from multivariate analyses that include a whole set of controls. In these models, we see that the misinformation coefficient in Model 3, where the dependent variable is affirmative action policy, also becomes negative and is significant at the $p < 0.10$ level, yet the misinformation coefficient in Model 6 loses its statistical significance. Racial resentment, ideology, and partisanship continue to have large and significant effects across the board, though no consistent story emerges for age, income, gender and education.

Next, we explore the possibility that misinformation is potentially unequal in its predictive power for all social groups. To determine whether this is the case, we used the same estimation strategy as described previously but estimate it separately for each social group – Black Americans, Muslim Americans, Latinos, Asian Americans, and White Americans. In the online Appendix, we first replicate the bivariate and multivariate analyses examining the relationship between the aggregate misinformation indicator and hostile racialized policy

---

[32] We calculated the marginal effects for our main variables of interest by setting all the remaining variables are their mean or mode. The estimates are available upon request from the authors.

Table 2 Effects of (disaggregated) political misinformation on preferences for restrictive racialized policies

	(1) Immigration (Agg) Preferences	(2) Muslim (Agg) Preferences	(3) Affirmative Action Preferences	(4) Environment Preferences	(5) Crime Preferences	(6) Welfare Preferences
Agg. undocumented knowledge misinformation	0.0384*** (0.00560)					
Agg. Muslim knowledge misinformation		0.0505*** (0.00372)				
Affirmative action policies misinformation			0.00656 (0.0459)			
Hazardous environment misinformation				−0.0236* (0.0108)		
Incarceration likelihood misinformation					0.451*** (0.0533)	
Welfare beneficiaries misinformation						0.207*** (0.0478)
N	4732	4732	3618	4732	4073	4010
adj. R^2/pseudo R^2	0.010	0.037	0.000	0.001	0.015	0.005

Standard errors in parentheses

+ $p < 0.10$, * $p < 0.05$, ** $p < 0.01$, *** $p < 0.001$

support among each social group subsample separately in Table A9 (online). This positive relationship persists in every instance and among every social group, though at times, statistical significance is lost. The one exception is with regard to the Latino, Asian, and White multivariate analyses where the dependent variable is support for affirmative action.

Table A10 (online) presents the results from both bivariate and multivariate analyses examining the relationship between disaggregated misinformation indicators and hostile policy support among the Black, Latino, Asian, Muslim, and White subsamples. The results suggest that misinformation continues to predict restrictive policy support for most policies, though statistical power is not always present. We observe a positive relationship between misinformation about immigration and the restrictive immigration policy for all groups in the bivariate and multivariate estimations. A similar pattern exists for all groups when we examine the bivariate and multivariate associations between misinformation about Muslim Americans and the restrictive policy targeting them. Turning to affirmative action policies, we observe a mixed and weak relationship between affirmative action misinformation and support for hostile affirmative action policies in the bivariate, though this relationship turns negative and remains insignificant when evaluating the multivariate relationship. The results for misinformation about welfare and the environment are also mixed and mostly insignificant for the groups. However, the relationship between crime misinformation and hostile crime policy support is positive for all bivariate and multivariate models, and significant for all groups except Whites.

Overall, the analyses presented demonstrates that those who are misinformed about socially stigmatized groups are more likely to support hostile policies that target these populations compared to those with lower levels of misinformation. Aggregate political knowledge about these communities appears to be a more consistent predictor of hostile policy support compared to disaggregated misinformation measures for some issues, like affirmative action or the environment, but this may also be a function of not having more than one specific measure of misinformation on these issues. While we observe some differences for the affirmative action and environment policies, no consistent patterns emerge.

Taking a step back at the bigger picture, these results raise serious concerns for how we study supporters of restrictive policies targeting the most marginalized communities. If reliance on unregulated news sources unconstrained by journalistic norms continues as is or even increases, the likelihood of exposure to misinformation or false news stories, which often play to fear through sensationalist coverage, will be high and politically consequential.

3.3 Misinformation and Candidate Support/Evaluation

Thus far, we have shown that misinformation is correlated with increased support for restrictive policies where marginalized social groups are the main target. Next, we examine whether misinformation about stigmatized social groups is also related to individuals' presidential vote choice. While partisanship is arguably the most important predictor in shaping vote choice as has been demonstrated in the extant scholarship, (e.g., Bartels, 2000), our findings as well as previous work has pointed out that misinformation is greater among conservatives, Republicans, Trump supporters and the far right (e.g., Allcott and Gentzkow, 2017; Grinberg et al., 2019; Nithyanand, Schaffner and Gill, 2017). Thus, we expect to find a statistically significant and positive relationship between misinformation levels and support for and favorable evaluations of Republican presidential candidates.

Our survey asked respondents to report who they supported in the 2016 presidential election as well as their prospective assessment for the 2020 presidential election. The latter question is a proxy for Trump support in the future, given that he was already the likely 2020 Republican nominee at the time the survey was fielded. Specifically, in measuring Trump support in 2016, respondents were asked "Regardless of whether you voted or not, which candidate did you most support for the 2016 presidential election?" Those who selected Donald Trump were coded as 1 and those who selected "Hillary Clinton," "Some other candidate," and "None of the candidates" were coded as 0. Respondents were also asked "If you were to vote in the 2020 presidential election, would you be more likely to vote for the Democratic or Republican nominee for President?" Those who selected "Republican" were coded 1 and those who selected "Democratic" or "Some other candidate" were coded value 0. In addition to these two questions, we also asked respondents to provide their assessment of Trump's handling of his job as President; the four response categories ranged from strongly approve to strongly disapprove, with higher values indicating greater approval.

There are two critiques that can be levied against any sort of examination of the link between misinformation and Trump or Republican candidate vote choice and assessment. First, there is the issue of endogeneity. It could very well be the case that Trump supporters or future Republican voters are more likely to be misinformed than not. This problem is certainly noteworthy and we raise it to urge caution. Second, these are self-reported measures, meaning that substantial social desirability bias likely exists, especially for questions about vote choice. Nonetheless, although these measures are self-reported, publicly available voter records are unable to provide us with this type of information.[33] As such, we are using the next best possible information to capture the relationship between misinformation and individuals' preferred candidate and their candidate assessment/approval.

Table 3 examines the relationship between aggregate political misinformation and Trump support in 2016 (Model 1), Republican presidential support (where Trump is the presumptive nominee) in 2020 (Model 2), as well as Trump's presidential approval ratings (Model 3). The models present results from multivariate regressions, but for the sake of brevity, only display the coefficient for the main independent variable: aggregate political misinformation. Even with a full suite of control variables, our key independent variable of interest – aggregate political misinformation – remains statistically significant. The predicted probability of aggregate misinformation (0–13) moving from the mean to the maximum value on Trump presidential support in 2016 results in a 19.5% increase in support, and grew to 22.2% in 2020. As the full models in Table A11 (online) demonstrate, the effect sizes for partisanship (Democrat and Independent) are the largest predictors for Trump support in 2016 and Republican candidate support in 2020. Yet at the same time, it is worth noting that misinformation about socially marginalized groups continues to exert some consistent predictive power on presidential vote choice. To the best of our knowledge, this is the first study to document such a relationship.

Table 3 Effects of political misinformation on candidate support/evaluation

	(1) Trump Support 2016	(2) Trump Vote 2020	(3) Trump Presidential Approval
Aggregate political misinformation	0.0828*** (0.0114)	0.0959*** (0.0124)	0.0607*** (0.00642)
N	3919	3919	3801
adj. R^2/pseudo R^2	0.378	0.496	0.373

Standard errors in parentheses
$^+ p < 0.10$, $^* p < 0.05$, $^{**} p < 0.01$, $^{***} p < 0.001$

---

[33] Publicly available records can only provide us with information on whether or not someone voted, but not who they voted for.

In addition, we find a positive relationship between being misinformed and strong approval ratings of Trump's job as President. Much like the finding about misinformation being positively correlated with voting for Trump, those who are highly misinformed about socially marginalized groups also hold the most favorable assessments of his job performance. However, it is worth keeping in mind that the predictive power of partisanship, social identity, and feelings of racial resentment is greater than it is for misinformation.

The patterns we uncover here indicate that one important avenue forward for future research is to examine whether its misinformation broadly that is tied to Republican candidate support/evaluation or rather misinformation specifically about out-groups in the polity. While our analysis is limited to misinformation about stigmatized social groups, it would also be relevant for future researchers to examine whether this relationship persists for Republican candidates in down-ballot races (e.g. Congress, Governor).

3.4 Discussion

Does misinformation about historically socially marginalized populations influence politics? This Section evaluated whether misinformation specific to these populations was statistically meaningful for shaping policies that also correspond to these groups. We built on the extant literature and selected policies that are related to minority populations in the United States, including: immigration, anti-Muslim policies, affirmative action, environment, crime, and welfare.

We find that misinformation about social groups is politically relevant for members of these groups. In addition to other traditional markers of policy attitudes and candidate support, such as partisanship and racial resentment, political misinformation about socially stigmatized groups continues to be significantly associated with an individuals' policy preferences. Political misinformation generally, as well as particularized misinformation about groups affected by specific issues, both independently operate to reduce support for policies that directly impact these groups, such as affirmative action, immigration, and a Muslim Ban.

These results indicate that a misinformed public detrimentally impacts the status of stigmatized social groups in American politics. Support for hostile policies that target vulnerable members of the policies exerts very real feedback consequences for the politicians who are elected to represent the interests and policy preferences of their constituents. Given that misinformation increases support for these detrimental policies, strategic and re-election motivated politicians are incentivized to respond by advocating for these policies in office.

Our analyses demonstrate that misinformation about these groups also matters for other political considerations. Not only are those who are increasingly misinformed more likely to support restrictive racialized policies, they were also more likely in 2016 to lend their support to Trump who ran on numerous platforms targeting stigmatized groups. Being misinformed is also linked to support for him in the 2020 Presidential election.

Together, these results suggest that misinformation about stigmatized social groups helps to explain support for a range of hostile policies that are currently some of the most salient issues in the polity today – immigration, crime, the environment, and government assistance. We also demonstrate how misinformation about these groups matters for explaining Republican presidential vote choice in 2016 and 2020. Misinformation, then, is not politically inconsequential, and can help to explain fundamental political actions such as who we cast our votes for on election day and what positions we take on a variety of issues. The fact that misinformation about socially marginalized groups pervades these core political behaviors should raise concern for whether policies that are detrimental to marginalized groups in our democracy accurately reflect the preferences of an informed citizenry.

4 Implications of a (Mis)Informed Public

Thus far, we have provided evidence that we hope has persuaded you that misinformation about socially marginalized groups is linked to some key political outcomes such as our political behavior and attitudes. We began this effort by first developing a comprehensive measure of misinformation, paying special attention to the public's knowledge about the policies that directly affect these populations, such as affirmative action and criminal justice. Unlike other studies on misinformation, which broadly assess misinformation about a number of topics whether they be racialized or not, we pay particular attention to misinformation about populations that are under-examined, but for whom we have reason to suspect that misinformation may be the most consequential. When misinformation about issues that pertain to groups, such as Asian Americans, Black Americans, Latinos, and Muslim Americans is pervasive, we find a relationship for restrictive public policies that harm these groups.

4.1 Does Being Informed Affect Policy Support?

Having established that misinformation about these groups is deleterious to these groups, one lingering question that we briefly consider here is whether being correctly informed about these populations reduces hostile policy attitudes affecting them. We examine whether being correctly informed matters for improving the status of the stigmatized populations we are interested in. Specifically, our analysis is similar to those in Section 3: we assess the link between being fully informed and support for restrictive racialized policy preferences. Theoretically, we hypothesize that being politically informed about stigmatized social groups should decrease restrictive policy support targeting these populations across a whole host of issues because understanding how these stigmatized social groups fare in different facets of the American sociopolitical system gives rise to an awareness of the positioning of these groups, which in turn lowers support for further pursuing policies that can ostracize or target them.

We first evaluate how being generally informed about social groups in the aggregate shapes policy support. Here, "general information" is defined as the number of policy-related knowledge questions that were answered *correctly*.[34] Table 4 presents regression results testing the bivariate association between aggregate political information and policy support. The results here indicate that the more "correct" factual information that individuals hold, as a whole, the less likely they are to support policies that harm stigmatized social groups. Across the board, we observe negative and significant effects on hostile policies pertaining to immigration, Muslim Americans, affirmative action, environment, crime, and welfare. The effect of information appears to exert the most predictive power in explaining attitudes toward crime. These findings provide a first cut affirmation of our first hypothesis, which predicted that greater levels of political knowledge would be associated with less-restrictive policy opinions.

Similar to the analyses we conducted when examining the relationship between being misinformed and support for hostile policies, Table A12 (online) tests whether the patterns we observe for the informed persist while controlling for the individuals' social group membership (e.g. Black American, Latino, Asian, White, or Muslim), age, education, income, partisanship, gender, ideology, and racial resentment. Even while controlling for a whole host of variables, we find that having more general political information is associated with reduced support for restrictive policies targeting social groups across each

---

[34] Refer to Section 2 for the different measures of knowledge.

Table 4 Effects of informed (aggregated) political information on preferences for restrictive racialized policies

	(1) Immigration (Agg) Preferences	(2) Muslim (Agg) Preferences	(3) Affirmative Action Preferences	(4) Environment Preferences	(5) Crime Preferences	(6) Welfare Preferences
Aggregate Political Knowledge	−0.0260***	−0.0288***	−0.0581***	−0.0293***	−0.133***	−0.0398***
	(0.00168)	(0.00149)	(0.0106)	(0.00183)	(0.0103)	(0.0102)
N	4732	4732	3618	4732	4073	4010
adj. R^2/pseudo R^2	0.048	0.073	0.007	0.052	0.038	0.004

Standard errors in parentheses

$+ p < 0.10$, $^* p < 0.05$, $^{**} p < 0.01$, $^{***} p < 0.001$

issue area, though the substantive size of the coefficients decreases slightly. Turning to other controls, we observe that Democrats and Independents are less likely than Republicans to support restrictive policies, though, surprisingly, the coefficients for these variables fail to consistently predict policy attitudes. In the same vein, conservatives are more likely than their liberal and moderate counterparts to support these policies. We do not observe persistent effects for gender, age or education, though those with more income become more supportive of these restrictive policies. The coefficients for our racial resentment variables exert very large and positive substantive effects, indicating that racial animus plays an important role in explaining restrictive policy preferences. Nonetheless, we underscore that even while controlling for this important predictor, general knowledge of social groups in the aggregate continues to significantly decrease restrictive policy support.

The effects of correct information on issue attitudes may matter more when it directly affects their own group. That is, it might be the case that Latinos who possess a considerable amount of knowledge on immigration would support relaxing existing immigration policies. To account for this possibility, Table A13 (online) displays the coefficient for "PK: Aggregate Political Information" when we run the same bivariate (Models 1, 3, 5, 7, 9, and 11) and multivariate regressions (Models 2, 4, 6, 8, 10, and 12) as in Tables 4 and A12 and restricts the samples to only those individuals in each social group. Being informed in the aggregate reduces support in the bivariate for racial and ethnic groups across the board, except in three instances, for Latinos and for Whites on affirmative action, and for Asians with welfare. Generally, however, the pattern of being informed about social groups improving policy preferences toward them appears to hold. Thus, as a first step, these results confirm the existence of a relationship between an increase in aggregate political knowledge about social groups and decreased support for restrictive policies, which also holds true when we estimate this statistical model for each social group (Whites, Black Americans, Latinos, Asian Americans, and Muslim Americans).

Next, we examine whether specific political information items that correspond more directly to the policies being asked change the nature of this relationship between political misinformation and restrictive policy support. In Table 5, the main independent variable changes form in each of the models, as highlighted in the previous section. In Model 1, we test the relationship between two political knowledge questions about immigration – (1) population size of the undocumented population and (2) number of legal immigrants in the United States – and policy support for the restrictive immigration aggregate variable. We observe a negative and significant relationship between the key independent

Table 5 Effects of informed (disaggregated) political knowledge on preferences for restrictive racialized policies

	(1) Immigration (Agg) Preferences	(2) Muslim (Agg) Preferences	(3) Affirmative Action Preferences	(4) Environment Preferences	(5) Crime Preferences	(6) Welfare Preferences
PK: Aggregate undocumented knowledge	−0.0201** (0.00707)					
PK: Aggregate Muslim knowledge		−0.0952*** (0.00467)				
PK: Legality of affirmative action policies			0.0894+ (0.0482)			
PK: Likelihood of living in a hazardous environment				−0.0585*** (0.00891)		
PK: Incarceration likelihood					−0.468*** (0.0445)	
PK: Welfare beneficiaries						−0.204*** (0.0514)
N	4732	4732	3618	4732	4073	4010
adj. R^2/pseudo R^2	0.001	0.081	0.001	0.009	0.024	0.004

Standard errors in parentheses

+ $p < 0.10$, * $p < 0.05$, ** $p < 0.01$, *** $p < 0.001$

variable and our outcome variable, indicating that political knowledge, particularly about immigration, is negatively associated with support for restrictive immigration policies. In Model 2, we employ an aggregate Muslim knowledge variable as our independent variable, operationalized as an additive measure of three political information questions about Muslims: (1) whether most terror attacks in the United States are conducted by Muslims, (2) estimated number of Muslims in America, and (3) the country which has the largest number of Muslims. Here we again observe a negative and significant relationship between aggregate Muslim information and support for restrictive policies targeting Muslims.

Turning next to Models 3–6, we disaggregate the independent variables to evaluate whether even more specific political knowledge items that directly relate to the policy items asked change the nature of this relationship. Specifically, Model 3 includes an indicator for political awareness about the legality of affirmative action policies, Model 4 includes a variable capturing political information about the likelihood of communities of color to live in hazardous environmental areas, Model 5 tests the link between political knowledge about the likelihood of incarceration of Black and Latino men and restrictive crime preferences, and Model 6 examines the association between political knowledge about the racial majority of public housing beneficiaries and restrictive welfare policy preferences. With the exception of Model 3 which examines affirmative action policies, we find that the negative and significant relationships persist between political knowledge and restrictive policy preferences.[35]

---

[35] We further evaluate whether these results hold in a multivariate regression controlling for a host of factors known to shape racialized policy support. Tables A12–A15 display these results. We observe that the negative and significant relationships between disaggregated political knowledge items and restrictive policy support observed in the bivariate regressions hold, with the exception of affirmative action. The race/social group indicators are negative in all instances except for Latinos and Asians (welfare preferences). Coefficient signs for income, education, age, and gender vary considerably across models, restricting our ability to draw conclusions about these variables. The coefficients for partisanship and ideology are in the expected direction, with conservatives being more supportive of the policies compared to their counterparts, and Democrats and Independents being significantly less supportive than Republicans. Importantly, racial resentment again plays a large and substantive role in shaping policy support, though the political misinformation indicators continue to retain their size and significance. When we explore within group heterogeneity, we observe that while the coefficient signs flip in a few instances (e.g. Asian Americans and Muslim Americans on immigration preferences, and Black Americans and Latinos on welfare), these changes do not rise to statistical significance, and therefore are inconclusive. Nonetheless, the subgroup results do highlight one important point: the positive coefficient for affirmative action political knowledge appears for each social group, indicating that affirmative action is a policy area that does not seem to be explained by political knowledge.

In this brief analysis, we find that an informed public supports policies that are more inclusive and less harmful to those who belong to a myriad of stigmatized groups. These additional results together indicate that the more political knowledge individuals have, both with respect to specific policy areas but also in the aggregate, the less supportive they are of hostile policies that target stigmatized groups. Being politically informed thus appears to matter for reducing support for policies that negatively touch stigmatized social groups across a wide range of issue areas.

4.2 Correcting Misinformation: (Lack of) Causal Evidence

One final question is whether policy attitudes can become less restrictive if misinformation about stigmatized groups is corrected. In other words, does updating citizens with correct political information reduce hostile policy support? Having more political information about a group can reduce the amount of stereotypical information being communicated about them. At the same time, the existing research suggests that misinformation may be difficult to correct and could potentially lead to long-lasting effects despite being discredited (Nyhan and Reifler, 2015). Moreover, research has previously demonstrated that providing information that counters stereotypes about stigmatized groups may improve group attitudes (e.g., Williamson, 2019).

To unpack this critical question, we conducted three survey experiments where we offer correct information on up to three issue areas, and then evaluate whether providing information meant to increase political knowledge significantly improves policy attitudes, compared to a control condition where respondents are not given any information. The first survey experiment was conducted on 809 Amazon Mechanical Turk respondents in September 2019. The second survey experiment was included at the end of the Lucid survey instruments, which we use in the main analysis, and was fielded on 4,732 participants between October to November 2019. Finally, we conducted our third survey experiment on 1,984 Amazon Mechanical Turk subjects in January 2020.[36]

To preview our results, our experimental treatment of correct information failed to yield any consistent patterns of shifts in policy support. When we turn to heterogeneous analyses, we find the most consistent effects of individuals supporting less hostile policies to be among those with high levels of

---

[36] Summary statistics for each of the survey instruments can be found in Table A16 (online).

Table 6 Experimental design

Study	Control No Info	Treatment 1 Environment	Treatment 2 Welfare	Treatment 3 Crime
1. September 2019 MTurk	✓ $n = 200$	✓ $n = 201$	✓ $n = 203$	✓ $n = 205$
2. October-November 2019 Lucid	✓ $n = 1{,}593$	✓ $n = 1{,}566$	✓ $n = 1{,}573$	
3. January 2019 MTurk	✓ $n = 656$	✓ $n = 667$	✓ $n = 661$	

racial resentment – more so than even among the misinformed – suggesting perhaps that while racial resentment is an important factor in shaping misinformation about stigmatized groups, this population is also open to updating their understanding about those communities.

Each survey experiment included at least three conditions: a control condition and two treatment conditions that provided respondents with facts relating to stigmatized social groups on two issues: the environment and welfare. In the first experiment, we also included a third treatment condition where respondents are given factual information about crime as an issue. Table 6 displays the experimental designs of the three studies, and the number of respondents who were randomized into each experimental condition. The control did not expose individuals to any factual information, and simply forwarded survey respondents to the post-test questions. The environment condition read as follows:[37]

> A recent study by the Environmental Protection Agency found that when looking at areas most affected by particulate air emissions, like soot, there were large disparities between communities differentiated by color and social strata. African Americans faced the highest impact, with the community facing a 54 percent higher health burden compared to the overall population, the study found. Non-white communities overall had a 28 percent higher health burden and those living under the poverty line had a 35 percent higher burden.

---

[37] Factual information for the environment condition https://thehill.com/policy/energy-environment/375289-epa-scientists-find-emissions-greater-impact-low-income-communities.

Respondents who were randomized into the welfare condition were exposed to the following information:[38]

> The vast majority of Americans receiving one of the six major forms of government assistance are children below the age of 18. Nearly half of all children in the U.S. – 46.7 percent – received some form of government assistance at some point during 2012, while about two in five American children on average received assistance in a given month during the same year. Meanwhile, white people comprise the greatest number of recipients; about 35 million white people participated in one of the six major government assistance programs that year compared to 24 million Hispanics and 20 million Blacks.

Finally, 205 respondents in the first study were also randomized into an additional treatment condition on crime, which read:[39]

> The racial and ethnic makeup of U.S. prisons continues to look substantially different from the demographics of the country as a whole. In 2017, Blacks represented 12 percent of the U.S. adult population but 33 percent of the sentenced prison population. Whites accounted for 64 percent of adults but 30 percent of prisoners. And while Hispanics represented 16 percent of the adult population, they accounted for 23 percent of inmates.

Each survey instrument also gauges support for several outcome variables pertaining specifically to the issue areas that align with the treatment conditions.[40] All three survey experiments ask the following two questions:

(1) Please indicate whether you strongly agree or strongly disagree with the following statement: "The US government needs to take action to reduce the environmental risks that disproportionately affect racial/ethnic minorities."
(2) Do you want to see Congress increase spending on welfare programs, decrease spending, or keep it about the same?

Responses to the first question, which serves as our primary outcome variable for the environment treatments, were captured on a 1–5 Likert scale ranging from strongly agree to strongly disagree, with higher values for less support for the proposed policy. Response options were rescaled to range from 0–1. The second question gauges support for increasing federal spending

---

[38] Factual information for the welfare condition was generated from an article at www.thoughtco.com/who-really-receives-welfare-4126592.

[39] Factual information about the crime condition came from the Pew Research Center, www.pewresearch.org/fact-tank/2019/04/30/shrinking-gap-between-number-of-blacks-and-whites-in-prison/.

[40] In each instance, "don't know" response options were coded as missing values.

on welfare. Here, responses are coded as 0 for an increase in spending or for keeping it the same, and a 1 for a decrease in spending, such that increasing values indicate more support for a hostile policy. Subjects in the first study were also asked the following question, which serves as our third outcome variable corresponding to the crime treatment:

(3) Which of the following approaches to lowering the crime rate in the United States comes closer to your own view – do you think: more money and effort should go to tackling the social and economic problems that lead to crime through better education and job training (or) more money and effort should go to deterring crime by improving law enforcement with more prisons, police and judges?

Those who select more on law enforcement are coded as 1 and those who select more on social problems are coded as 0, to indicate that greater policy support is more hostile to marginalized social groups.

In developing these experiments, we hypothesized that exposure to correct factual information would reduce hostile policy support in the aggregate. Nonetheless, we expected experimental effects to be less pronounced among populations who typically have lower levels of misinformation about these groups already, such as Democrats and those with low levels of racial resentment, because the information in the treatments will likely not cause them to update their priors and become even less supportive of these policies. In other words, we may observe a floor effect among these populations. In turn, we expected larger effects among those with higher levels of racial resentment and Republicans, because they constitute segments of the population that are more likely to be misinformed, and for whom the presentation of new information might actually be novel and counter to the information they typically are exposed to about these populations.

4.2.1 Aggregate Experimental Results

To begin, we present aggregate experimental effects (e.g. differences in means between our relevant treatment conditions) in Table 7.[41] First, we evaluate effects on our outcome variable about the environment, examining differences across the three studies between: (1) the environment treatment and the other treatment condition(s) and control, (2) the environment treatment and the control, and (3) the control condition and the treatments. We find statistically significant effects in Study 2 for the first two analyses; these estimates are denoted in blue. What these results suggest is that those exposed to the

---

[41] Note that entries in blue denote statistically significant effects at the $p < 0.1$ level.

Table 7. Aggregate Experimental Effects

Study	Diff-in-means analysis	Treatment mean	Comparison group mean	Diff	P-value
		Effects on Environment			
Study 1	Environment v. All	0.3010	0.3039	0.0029	$p = 0.9133$
Study 1	Environment v. Control	0.3010	0.2984	-0.0026	$p = 0.9373$
Study 1	Control v. All	0.2985	0.3049	0.0064	$p = 0.8099$
Study 2	**Environment v. All**	**0.3225**	**0.3410**	**0.0185**	**p = 0.0516**
Study 2	**Environment v. Control**	**0.3225**	**0.3416**	**0.0192**	**p = 0.0781**
Study 2	Control v. All	0.3416	0.3314	-0.0102	$p = 0.2783$
Study 3	Environment v. All	0.2942	0.3077	0.0135	$p = 0.3531$
Study 3	Environment v. Control	0.2942	0.3128	0.0186	$p = 0.2706$
Study 3	Control v. All	0.3128	0.2984	-0.0144	$p = 0.3256$
		Effects on Welfare			
Study 1	**Welfare v. All**	**0.1684**	**0.2487**	**0.0802**	**p = 0.0244**
Study 1	**Welfare v. Control**	**0.1685**	**0.2396**	**0.0711**	**p = 0.0881**
Study 1	Control v. All	0.2396	0.2256	-0.0140	$p = 0.6905$
Study 2	Welfare v. All	0.2073	0.2124	0.0051	$p = 0.7101$
Study 2	Welfare v. Control	0.2073	0.2136	0.0063	$p = 0.6873$
Study 2	Control v. All	0.2136	0.2092	-0.0044	$p = 0.7440$
Study 3	Welfare v. All	0.2606	0.2596	-0.0011	$p = 0.9614$
Study 3	Welfare v. Control	0.2606	0.2559	-0.0047	$p = 0.8519$
Study 3	Control v. All	0.2559	0.2619	0.0060	$p = 0.7862$
		Effects on Crime			
Study 1	Crime v. All	0.1881	0.1864	-0.0018	$p = 0.9568$
Study 1	Crime v. Control	0.1882	0.1719	-0.0163	$p = 0.6810$
Study 1	Control v. All	0.1719	0.1920	0.0201	$p = 0.5378$

treatment condition were less likely to support the hostile policy more than the other treatment and control combined ($p = 0.0516$), and also significantly less likely to support the policy compared to the control only ($p = 0.0781$). In no other instance did exposure to our treatment cause respondents to significantly change their policy support for the environment policy.

Next, we evaluate whether our treatments caused any shifts on support for the adoption of restrictive welfare policy. Similar to the analysis involving the environment treatments, we conducted three sets of analyses, where we examine the difference in means in support for the welfare policy between experimental conditions, across each of the three experiments: (1) the welfare treatment and the other treatment condition(s) and control, (2) the welfare treatment and the control, and (3) the control condition and the treatments. In this instance, we only observed significant effects for the first two analyses in Study 1; those in the welfare treatment were significantly less likely to support the policy compared to the other treatments and control ($p = 0.0244$), as well as when compared only to respondents in the control condition ($p = 0.0881$). These findings do not replicate in the aggregate in Studies 2 and 3.

Finally, we examine whether exposure to the treatment on crime significantly affected respondents' support for a hostile policy on crime compared to experimental conditions about the environment, welfare, and a control in Study 1 only. In this instance, we find no statistically significant difference for the crime policy dependent variable when we compare: (1) the crime treatment to the other two treatments and the control; (2) the crime treatment to the control only; and (3) the control to all of the treatments. As such, we conclude that our treatment on crime failed to move individuals to hold less restrictive policy positions on crime.

Overall, these results indicate the lack of any consistent pattern of the main effects from our three experimental studies. While we have significant differences across Studies 1 and 2 in two distinct instances (e.g. Study 1 and effects on welfare, and Study 2 and effects on the environment), these aggregate results do not replicate across any additional studies. Next, we turn to heterogeneous results to examine whether we observe experimental effects among certain subsets of respondents.

4.2.2 Heterogeneous Treatment Effects

Though we do not observe any consistent aggregate experimental effects, our findings from Section 2 lead us to expect that certain subsets of the population may be more amenable to factual information, which in turn causes them to be less supportive of hostile policies. On the one hand, we may expect Democrats and those low on racial resentment to be amenable to the information provided in the factual treatments, given that they score low on misinformation. On the other hand, we may expect very little effect of our treatments on these two subsets of the population, precisely because they score low on misinformation and are already not likely to support the proposed hostile policies. In contrast, we expect those high on racial resentment and Republicans to be more persuadable by our information treatments because, as the results from Section 2 indicate, these groups constitute segments of the population that are susceptible to misinformation to begin with. Additionally, the presentation of new information might actually be novel to these subsets of individuals and counter to the information they typically are exposed to about these populations.

We begin by first examining whether our treatments are more powerful among the misinformed than in the aggregate. Table A17 (online) displays the key analyses in black and the secondary analyses in grey. Specifically, we conduct the same difference-in-means test as in Table 7, though we now examine whether these effects hold among the misinformed on the specific topic that pertains to the specific treatment at hand. For instance, the pertinent analysis in the first section examines the effect of the environment treatment on the hostile environment policy, among those who are misinformed about the environment. We find no significant differences between treatments and the control when examining the welfare and environment treatments in Studies 1, 2, and 3. Turning to the crime treatment, we do not observe significant differences in Study 1 for our main analysis among those who are misinformed about incarceration and crime, but we do see them for those who are misinformed about the environment. These findings, however, do not provide empirical support that our treatments meaningfully shaped policy support among the misinformed.

Next, we turn to an analysis among Democrats and among respondents with low racial resentment on the left- and right-hand side of Table A18 (online). respectively. No differential patterns emerge for Democratic respondents, though we do observe some effects in Study 3 for the welfare treatment ($p < 0.10$). Nonetheless, given our inability to replicate the patterns here, we conclude that our treatments were not powerful among this subset of the population.

Finally, we test whether our treatments altered policy attitudes for Republicans and those with high racial resentment. Table A18 displays these results. We observe significant differences among those who were exposed to the environment treatment and the other conditions among those with high racial resentment in Studies 2 and 3. Similarly, the effects of partisanship, namely amongst Republicans, emerge in Study 3; it is also worth highlighting that partisanship almost reaches statistical significance in Study 2. The patterns become less consistent for the welfare treatment. The differences are significant at times for this condition among those with high racial resentment in Studies 2 and 3, while they appear to only matter for Republican respondents in Study 1. No significant differences emerge for the crime treatment for either subset.

Our three studies provide minimal causal evidence that informing respondents with factual information about stigmatized groups alters policy attitudes affecting these populations. These results are in line with Wallace and Zepeda-Millán (2020) work, which finds that even when information about immigration is corrected, Republicans do not update their priors. We do, however, observe the greatest consistent effects amongst those possessing high amounts of racial resentment, where the environment and welfare treatments significantly different from the other experimental conditions in Studies 2 and 3.

We recognize that the inconsistency of these results makes it difficult to draw any strong causal conclusions from our studies. Rather, we urge future experimental work to select issues that the public would know less about, such as transportation or health, rather than issues that are rather salient and saturated in the mainstream debate, such as welfare, the environment, and crime. It may also be the case that future studies would benefit from the use of a more direct and overt treatment; perhaps explicitly stating an incorrect fact, and then with a follow-up statement that provides the correct information would cause a significant shift in one's policy attitudes.

One additional possible explanation for why we may not be observing movement on our dependent variable is that our treatment may not be linked strongly enough with our dependent variables. While providing respondents with correct information may not make them less restrictive on racialized policy issues, though it could potentially change their ratings of these groups. Although our study is more concerned with political outcomes, evaluations of stigmatized outcomes could also be an area worth further exploration. Finally, we acknowledge the difficulty in correcting for misinformation that would actually result in any meaningful policy change, which is consistent with previous work (Nyhan and Reifler, 2010; Wallace and Zepeda-Millán, 2020).

4.3 Broader Implications

This Element sought to narrow the scholarly focus on misinformation broadly to misinformation about specific marginalized social groups. In not only assessing how much misinformation tends to exist about groups, such as Black Americans, Latinos, Asian Americans, and Muslim Americans, we also demonstrate that this type of misinformation is consequential insofar as it shapes the general public's support for hostile policies targeting these populations.

First, we fill the misinformation knowledge gap by probing the public about their awareness of factual information pertaining to socially marginalized groups, such as the size of the undocumented immigrant population in the nation, and current and future projections about the ethnic/racial composition of the country. We also asked survey respondents to provide their knowledge of Muslim Americans, relating to their population size, country of origin, and other "factual" questions. Such efforts, we hoped, would provide an important baseline for just how much or how little the American public knows about these socially marginalized groups and to gauge the degree of misinformation that is out there. Our study uncovers that levels of misinformation about Asian Americans, Black Americans, Latinos, Muslim Americans, and immigrants are fairly profound and even more pronounced across certain segments of the public. Being misinformed depends on one's own social identity, source for news, racial attitudes, and where one falls on the left-right ideological scale. White Americans, along with those who are racially resentful, ideologically conservative, and consumers of conservative news outlets are particularly vulnerable to being misinformed about socially marginalized groups. All told, misinformation about socially marginalized groups is uneven in the American citizenry.

Second, after establishing these baseline levels of misinformation, we then turn our attention to addressing the "why do we care" question. That is, what, if any, are the political consequences of holding incorrect information about Muslim Americans and ethnic/racial minorities? In a nutshell, our empirical analyses demonstrate that the misinformed possess more hostile attitudes on racialized policies. That is, overestimating the number of undocumented immigrants in the United States is correlated to increased support for restrictive immigration measures (e.g. building a border wall, or limiting the number of immigrants admitted in the country). We also go on to uncover the role of misinformation on voter decision-making. Namely, we find a similar pattern between misinformation and holding a more conservative political viewpoint. In the case of voter choice, being misinformed is correlated with greater support for Trump in the 2016 and the 2020 presidential election. Taken altogether, our results lend support to our claim that misinformation about socially marginalized groups is not without serious political ramifications. Finally, we conducted three different experimental studies in an effort to determine whether correct information causes a change in policy preferences. The results from these studies yield a rather inconsistent and inconsequential set of estimates, therefore limiting our ability to clearly identify the casual role of information on policy attitudes. Nonetheless, our observational analyses provide us with ample evidence to conclude that the political consequences of misinformation are, by and large, negative. Being misinformed is associated with a tendency to support policies that make socially and politically vulnerable groups in the United States worse off.

Our findings speak to the larger literature on misinformation and political knowledge more generally. To have a functional and well-running democracy, citizens are expected to be informed and aware participants in the political process. It also calls on the public to stay abreast of pressing issues and current events as well have a good understanding of the overall political process.

Yet in an era where the public struggles between dissecting what is "real" news and what is "fake news," the goal of having an aware and informed citizenry can sometimes feel insurmountable. Moreover, for those in the public who engage in directionally motivated reasoning, such efforts at curbing misinformation may be even more difficult. Yet this does not mean that we should abandon all sense of hope or optimism. As Hochschild and Einstein (2015*b*) write, change is possible. Some of the strategies that they offer to move individuals out of a state of misinformation "range from education to persuasion to shaming, and from confronting citizens directly to working around them through experts or rules," p. 624. These strategies offer some optimism that the high rates of misinformation and fake news that currently dominate the US landscape can be rectified. Our findings offer some glimmer of hope as well. Individuals who are knowledgeable about marginalized social groups, both with respect to specific policy areas but also at the aggregate level, tend to reduce their support for restrictive policies targeting stigmatized groups. Thus, being politically engaged and aware is politically consequential as well, and this case, we find that it reduces support for policies that negatively touch stigmatized social groups across a wide range of issue areas.

As other studies have pointed out (e.g. see Lewandowsky et al., 2017), correcting the misinformed in the era of "fake news" and "post-truth," is not an easy task. Lewandowsky, Ecker, and Cook (2017) suggest that the solution "must involve technological solutions incorporating psychological principles, an interdisciplinary approach that we describe as technocognition."

A further complication is brought to bear in Schaffner and Luks's (2018) study. They uncover that some of the misinformation that arises in survey responses is not only a function of misinformed views, but it can also take the form of "partisan cheerleading." When they asked respondents to estimate the relative sizes of crowds at Donald Trump's and Barack Obama's presidential inaugurations, they found evidence of expressive responding, particularly amongst partisans with high levels of political engagement. Thus, disentangling the truly misinformed from the partisan or ideologue, or in our case, the racially resentful, remains an ongoing issue for survey researchers. Our intuition is that amongst those who hold most animosity toward socially marginalized groups, any sort of correction may prove to be in vain. One possible way to disentangle those who engage in "partisan cheerleading" versus those who are truly misinformed is to design an experiment where subjects are provided some form of an incentive (e.g. monetary), for providing the correct response.

Should incentives not be enough, however, to reduce misinformation about socially marginalized groups, this would raise a series of concerns. Latinos, Muslim Americans, and Jews are being disproportionately targeted online with disinformation, harassment, and computational propaganda.[42] Arguably then, these misinformation attacks may be fostering an inhospitable atmosphere for marginalized individuals in the United States: according to a recent study, 27% of Black Americans, 30% of Latino, and 35% of Muslim Americans, and 63% members have experienced harassment online due to their identity.[43]

4.3.1 Future Research Avenues

As with all social science research, ours is not without limitations. Ideally, we would have liked to conduct our experiments on a larger range of issue areas, field the survey in several languages, and develop alternative experimental designs, such as using a randomized block design based on respondents' misinformation levels. Due to resource constraints, our study also does not include samples of Indigenous/American Indians, about whom misinformation is at least anecdotally, quite high.

Moreover, future research efforts should not only unpack what factual interventions may lessen hostile policy support toward groups, particularly among the misinformed, but also consider the role of media outlets themselves. Arguably, news media outlets that perpetuate and propagate misinformation are one source of the problem. What incentives do they have to provide more accurate news making? If they are driven by profit, perhaps not much. If prior levels of misinformation are indeed theoretically important for expecting shifts in policy attitudes, then designing experiments that block randomize on misinformation levels may also be informative.

Scholarship would also be well-served to understand what kinds of misinformation actually exist in the news media on policy domains relating to stigmatized groups. While our study does not address this, certainly future work would be well-advised to do so, particularly since we have documented such a relationship in our study.

---

[42] www.iftf.org/fileadmin/user_upload/downloads/ourwork/IFTF_Executive_Summary_ comp.prop_W_05.07.19_01.pdf

[43] www.adl.org/onlineharassment

It also remains to be seen just how much misinformation about stigmatized groups *actually* exists in the public and whether and how it spreads, especially on social media. Studies evaluating just how much misinformation about marginalized groups circulates social media will enable us to develop a deeper understanding of just pervasive it is.

Moreover, our study has developed several measures of misinformation specifically pertaining to several groups. Yet additional measures of misinformation about these and other socially marginalized groups, such as about the LGBTQ+ community and American Jews, can be developed and tested as well.[44] Future work could also assess additional political factors in addition to policy attitudes, namely to explore whether providing factual information shifts individuals' behaviors, such as through the information they would share with co-partisans (e.g. Carlson, 2019). Finally, while our existing study makes inroads into unpacking how and in what ways misinformation matters for politics, there is still much to learn. We hope our initial efforts motivate and inspires other researchers to delve deeper into the causes and consequences of misinformation for vulnerable groups.

---

[44] Ideally, we would have liked to include Indigneous/American Indians as part of our study, though due to resource constraints, we were unable to do so.

Bibliography

Abrajano, Marisa A. 2015. "Reassessing the racial gap in political knowledge." *Journal of Politics* 77(1):44–54.

Abrajano, Marisa and Zoltan L Hajnal. 2015. *White backlash: Immigration, race, and American politics.* Princeton University Press.

Ahler, Douglas J. and Gaurav Sood. 2018. "The parties in our heads: Misperceptions about party composition and their consequences." *The Journal of Politics* 80(3):964–981.
URL: *https://doi.org/10.1086/697253*

Allcott, Hunt and Matthew Gentzkow. 2017. "Social media and fake news in the 2016 election." *Journal of Economic Perspectives* 31(2):211–236.

Allport, Gordon. 1954. *The Nature of Prejudice.* Basic Books.

Anspach, Nicolas M. and Taylor N. Carlson. 2018. "What to believe? Social media commentary and belief in misinformation." *Political Behavior* pp. 1–22.

Aziz, Sahar F. 2017. "A Muslim registry: The precursor to internment." *BYU Law Review* p. 779.

Barberá, Pablo. 2018. Explaining the spread of misinformation on social media: Evidence from the 2016 US presidential election. In *Symposium: Fake News and the Politics of Misinformation. American Political Science Association Comparative Politics Newsletter.*

Barkan, Steven E. and Steven F. Cohn. 2005. "Why whites favor spending more money to fight crime: The role of racial prejudice." *Social Problems* 52(2):300–314.

Bartels, Larry M. 1996. "Uninformed votes: Information effects in presidential elections." *American Journal of Political Science* pp. 194–230.

Bartels, Larry M. 2000. "Partisanship and voting behavior, 1952–1996." *American Journal of Political Science* pp. 35–50.

Benegal, Salil D. 2018. "The spillover of race and racial attitudes into public opinion about climate change." *Environmental Politics* 27(4):733–756.

Berelson, Bernard R., Paul F. Lazarsfeld, and William N. McPhee. 1954. *Voting: A Study of Opinion Formation in a Presidential Campaign.* University of Chicago Press.

Berg, Charles Ramirez. 1990. "Stereotyping in films in general and of the Hispanic in particular." *Howard Journal of Communications* 2(3): 286–300.

Berg, Charles Ramirez. 2002. *Latino Images in Film: Stereotypes, Subversion and Resistance*. University of Texas Press.

Berinsky, Adam. 2015. "Rumors and health care reform: Experiments in political misinformation." *British Journal of Political Science* 47(2):241–262.

Bobo, Lawrence D. and Devon Johnson. 2004. "A taste for punishment: Black and white Americans' views on the death penalty and the war on drugs." *Du Bois Review: Social Science Research on Race* 1(1):151–180.

Bobo, Lawrence D., Melvin L. Oliver, Jr., James H. Johnson and Valenzuela Abel, Jr. 2000. *Prismatic Metropolis: Inequality in Los Angeles*. Russell Sage Foundation.

Bonilla-Silva, Eduardo. 2015. *The Structure of Racism in color-blind, "post-racial" America*. Sage Publications: Los Angeles, CA.

Boussalis, Constantine and Travis G. Coan. 2017. "Elite polarization and correcting misinformation in the "post-truth era" Journal of Applied Research in Memory and Cognition. 6(4): 405–408.".

Budak, Ceren, Sharad Goel and Justin M. Rao. 2016. "Fair and balanced? Quantifying media bias through crowdsourced content analysis." *Public Opinion Quarterly* 80(S1):250–271.

Calfano, Brian. 2018. *Muslims, Identity, and American Politics*. Routledge.

Calfano, Brian Robert, Nazita Lajevardi and Melissa R. Michelson. 2017. "Trumped up challenges: limitations, opportunities, and the future of political research on Muslim Americans." *Politics, Groups, and Identities* pp. 1–11.

Campbell, Angus, Philip E. Converse, Warren E. Miller and Donald E. Stokes. 1960. *The American Voter*. University of Chicago Press.

Carlson, Matt. 2018. "Fake news as an informational moral panic: the symbolic deviancy of social media during the 2016 US presidential election." *Information, Communication & Society* pp. 1–15.

Carlson, Taylor, Marisa Abrajano and Lisa Garcia Bedolla. 2020. *Talking Politics: Political Discussion Networks and the New American Electorate*. Oxford University Press.

Carlson, Taylor N. 2019. "Through the grapevine: Informational consequences of interpersonal political communication." *American Political Science Review* 113(2):325–339.

Cassiman, Shawn A. 2008. "Resisting the neo-liberal poverty discourse: On constructing deadbeat dads and welfare queens." *Sociology Compass* 2(5):1690–1700.

Chakraborty, Jayajit, Juliana A Maantay and Jean D Brender. 2011. "Dispro-portionate proximity to environmental health hazards: Methods, models, and measurement." *American Journal of Public Health* 101(S1):S27–S36.

Chavez, Leo Ralph. 2001. *Covering Immigration: Popular Images and the Politics of the Nation.* University of California Press Berkeley.

Chavez, Leo. 2008. *The Latino Threat: Constructing Immigrants, Citizens and the Nation.* Stanford University Press.

Chavez, Leo. 2013. *The Latino threat: Constructing Immigrants, Citizens, and the Nation.* Stanford University Press.

Cohen, Cathy J. 1999. *The Boundaries of Blackness: AIDS and the Breakdown of Black Politics.* University of Chicago Press.

Collingwood, Loren, Nazita Lajevardi and Kassra AR Oskooii. 2018. "A change of heart? Why individual-level public opinion shifted against Trump's 'Muslim Ban'." *Political Behavior* 40(4):1035–1072.

Collins, Patricia Hill. 2002. *Black Feminist Thought: Knowledge, Conscious-ness, and the Politics of Empowerment.* Routledge.

Dahl, Robert. 1971. "Polyarchy: participation and opposition." *New Haven.*

Dahl, Robert Alan. 1989. *Democracy and Its Critics.* Yale University Press.

Dalisay, Francis and Alexis Tan. 2009. "Assimilation and contrast effects in the priming of Asian American and African American stereotypes through TV exposure." *Journalism and Mass Communication Quarterly* 86(1):7–22.

Davis, Joshua T. 2019. "Funding God's policies, defending whiteness: Chris-tian nationalism and whites' attitudes towards racially-coded government spending." *Ethnic and Racial Studies* 42(12):2123–2142.

Dawson, Michael C. 1995. *Behind the Mule: Race and Class in African-American Politics.* Princeton University Press.

DellaVigna, Stefano and Ethan Kaplan. 2007. "The Fox News effect: Media bias and voting*." *The Quarterly Journal of Economics* 122(3):1187–1234.
URL: *https://doi.org/10.1162/qjec.122.3.1187*

Delli Carpini, Michael X. Delli and Scott Keeter. 1996. *What Americans Know about Politics and Why It Matters.* Yale University Press.

Dovidio, J. F., and Gaertner S. L. (eds.). 1986. *Prejudice, Discrimination, and Racism.* Academic Press.

Druckman, James N. 2004. "Political preference formation: Competition, deliberation, and the (Ir)relevance of framing effects." *American Political Science Review* 98(4):671–686.

Druckman, James N. and Kjersten R. Nelson. 2003. "Framing and delibera-tion: How citizens' conversations limit elite influence." *American Journal of Political Science* 47(4):729–745.
URL: *https://onlinelibrary.wiley.com/doi/abs/10.1111/1540-5907.00051*

Enders, Adam M and Jamil S Scott. 2019. "The increasing racialization of American electoral politics, 1988–2016." *American Politics Research* 47(2):275–303.

Enos, Ryan D. 2014. "Causal effect of intergroup contact on exclusionary attitudes." *Proceedings of the National Academy of Sciences* 111(10): 3699–3704.

URL: *www.pnas.org/content/111/10/3699*

Eric Oliver, J and Janelle Wong. 2003. "Intergroup prejudice in multiethnic settings." *American journal of political science* 47(4):567–582.

Farkas, Johan and Jannick Schou. 2018. "Fake news as a floating signifier: Hegemony, antagonism and the politics of falsehood." *Javnost – The Public* 25(3):298–314.

URL: *https://doi.org/10.1080/13183222.2018.1463047*

Farris, Emily M. and Heather Silber Mohamed. 2018. "Picturing immigration: How the media criminalizes immigrants." *Politics, Groups, and Identities* 6(4):814–824.

URL: *https://doi.org/10.1080/21565503.2018.1484375*

Fearon, James D. 1999. "Electoral accountability and the control of politicians: selecting good types versus sanctioning poor performance." *Democracy, Accountability, and Representation* 55:61.

Flynn, D. J., Brendan Nyhan and Jason Reifler. 2017. "The nature and origins of misperceptions: Understanding false and unsupported beliefs about politics." *Political Psychology* 38:127–150.

Fong, Timothy. 1998. *The Contemporary Asian American Experience: Beyond the Model Minority*. Prentice Hall.

Fujioka, Yuki. 1999. "Television portrayals and African-American stereotypes: Examination of television effects when direct contact is lacking." *Journalism and Mass Communication Quarterly* 76(1):52–75.

García Bedolla, Lisa. 2005. *Fluid Borders: Latino Power, Identity, and Politics in Los Angeles*. Univ of California Press.

García Bedolla, Lisa. 2015. *Latino Politics*. Polity: UK.

Ghandoosh, Nazgol. 2019. "U.S. prison population trends: Massive Buildup and Modest Decline." Briefing Paper.

URL: *www.sentencingproject.org/publications/u-s-prison-population-trends-massive-buildup-and-modest-decline/*

Gil de Zúñiga, Homero, Teresa Correa and Sebastian Valenzuela. 2012. "Selective exposure to cable news and immigration in the U.S.: The relationship between FOX News, CNN, and attitudes toward Mexican immigrants." *Journal of Broadcasting and Electronic Media* 56(4):597–615.

URL: *https://doi.org/10.1080/08838151.2012.732138*

Gilens, Martin. 1996. "Race coding" and white opposition to welfare." *American Political Science Review* 90(3):593–604.

Gilens, Martin. 2001. "Political ignorance and collective policy preferences." *American Political Science Review* 95(2):379–396.

Gilens, Martin. 2009. *Why Americans Hate Welfare: Race, Media, and the Politics of Antipoverty Policy*. University of Chicago Press.

Giliam, Frank and Shanto Iyengar. 2000. "Prime suspects: The influence of local television news on the viewing public." *American Journal of Political Science*. 44(3): 560–573.

Gilliam, Jr., Franklin D. 1999. "The "welfare queen" experiment." *Nieman Reports* 53(2):49.

Gilliam, Jr., Franklin D., Shanto Iyengar, Adam Simon and Oliver Wright. 1996. "Crime in black and white: The violent, scary world of local news." *Harvard International Journal of Press/Politics* 1(3):6–23.

Goldberg, David Theo. 2002. *The Racial State*. Blackwell Publishing.

Gonzalez O'Brien, Benjamin, Matt A. Barreto and Gabriel R. Sanchez. 2020. "They're all out to get me! Assessing inter-group competition among multiple populations." *Politics, Groups, and Identities* 8(5):867–893.

Green, Donald, Bradley Palmquist and Eric Schickler. 2002. *Partisan Hearts and Minds: Political Parties and the Social Identities of Voters*. Yale University Press.

Green, Eva G. T., Christian Staerkle and David O. Sears. 2006. "Symbolic racism and Whites' attitudes towards punitive and preventive crime policies." *Law and Human Behavior* 30(4):435–454.

Greenberg, Bradley S., Dana Mastro and Jeffrey E. Brand. 2002. "Minorities and the mass media: Television into the 21st century." *Media effects: Advances in Theory and Research* pp. 333–351.

Grinberg, Nir, Kenneth Joseph, Lisa Friedland, Briony Swire-Thompson and David Lazer. 2019. "Fake news on Twitter during the 2016 US presidential election." *Science* 363(6425):374–378.

Gutierrez, Lorraine M. 1995. "Understanding the empowerment process: Does consciousness make a difference?" *Social Work Research* 19(4):229–237.

Hamamoto, Darrell Y. 1994. *Monitored Peril: Asian Americans and the Politics of TV Representation*. University of Minnesota Press.

Harris, Allison P., Hannah L. Walker and Laurel Eckhouse. 2020. "No justice, no peace: political science perspectives on the American carceral state." *Journal of Race, Ethnicity and Politics* 5(3):427–449.

Hochschild, Jennifer and Katherine Levine Einstein. 2015*a*. "'It isn't what we don't know that gives us trouble, it's what we know that ain't so': Misinformation and democratic politics." *British Journal of Political Science* 45(3):467–475.

Hochschild, Jennifer L. and Katherine Levine Einstein. 2015*b*. *Do facts matter?: Information and misinformation in American politics*. Vol. 13. University of Oklahoma Press.

Huckfeldt, Robert and John Sprague. 1987. "Networks in context: The social flow of political information." *American Political Science Review* 81(4):1197–1216.

Hunt, Darnell and Ana-Christina Ramon. 2010. *Black Los Angeles: American dreams and racial realities*. New York University Press.

Hunt, Darnell M. 1999. *OJ Simpson facts and fictions: News rituals in the construction of reality*. Cambridge University Press.

Hunt, Darnell M. 2005. *Channeling blackness: Studies on television and race in America*. Oxford University Press, USA.

Hurwitz, Jon and Mark Peffley. 2005. "Playing the race card in the post–Willie Horton era: The impact of racialized code words on support for punitive crime policy." *Public Opinion Quarterly* 69(1):99–112.

Jackson, Jenn M. 2019. "Black Americans and the "crime narrative": comments on the use of news frames and their impacts on public opinion formation." *Politics, Groups, and Identities* 7(1):231–241.

Jamal, Amaney. 2009. "The Racialization of Muslim Americans." *Muslims in Western Politics* pp. 200–215.

Jardina, Ashley and Michael Traguott. 2019. "The genesis of the birther rumor: Partisanship, racial attitudes, and political knowledge." *Journal of Race, Ethnicity and Politics* 4(1):60–80.

Jones-Correa, Michael. 1998. *Between two nations: The political predicament of Latinos in New York City*. Cornell University Press.

Jost, J. T., Glaser, J. Kruglanski A. W., and Sulloway, F. J. 2003. "Political conservatism as motivated social cognition." *Psychological Bulletin* 129(3):339–375.

Junn, Jane and Natalie Masuoka. 2008. "Asian American identity: Shared racial status and political context." *Perspectives on Politics* pp. 729–740.

Key, V. O. 1966. *The responsible electorate*. Harvard University Press.

Kim, Claire Jean. 1999. "The racial triangulation of Asian Americans." *Politics & Society* 27(1):105–138.

Kim, Claire Jean. 2000. "Playing the racial trump card: Asian Americans in contemporary US politics." *Amerasia Journal* 26(3):35–65.

Kim, Claire Jean. 2018. "Are Asians the New Blacks?: Affirmative action, anti-blackness, and the 'sociometry' of race." *Du Bois Review: Social Science Research on Race* 15(2):217–244.

Kim, Minjeong and Angie Chung. 2005. "Consuming orientalism: Images of Asian/American women in multicultural advertising." *Qualitative Sociology* 28(1):67–91.

Kinder, Donald and David O. Sears. 1981. "Prejudice and politics: Symbolic racism versus racial threats to the good life." *Journal of Personality and Social Psychology,* 40(3):414–431.

Kinder, Donald and Kalmoe, Nathan P. 2017. *Neither Liberal nor Conservative: Ideological innocence in the American public.* Chicago: University of Chicago Press.

Kinder, Donald and Lynn M. Sanders. 1996. *Divided by race: Racial politics and democratic ideals.* University of Chicago Press.

Klofstad, Casey A. 2010. "The Lasting Effect of Civic Talk on Civic Participation: Evidence from a Panel Study." *Social Forces* 88(5):2353–2375. **URL:** *https://doi.org/10.1353/sof.2010.0047*

Kozlovic, Anton Karl. 2007. "Islam, Muslims and Arabs in the popular Hollywood cinema." *Comparative Islamic Studies* 3(2):213–246.

Kuklinski, James H., Paul J. Quirk, Jennifer Jerit, David Schwieder and Robert F. Rich. 2000. "Misinformation and the currency of democratic citizenship." *Journal of Politics* 62(3):790–816.

Lajevardi, Nazita. 2020. *Outsiders at home: The politics of American Islamophobia.* Cambridge University Press.

Lajevardi, Nazita. 2021. "The media matters: Muslim American Portrayals and the Effects on Mass Attitudes." *The Journal of Politics* Forthcoming, 2021. **URL:** *https://www.journals.uchicago.edu/doi/10.1086/711300*

Lajevardi, Nazita, Kassra A. R. Oskooii and Hannah L Walker. 2020. "Social Media Information Consumption and Support for Anti-Muslim American Policy Proposals." Working Paper.

Lajevardi, Nazita and Marisa Abrajano. 2019. "How negative sentiment toward Muslim Americans predicts support for Trump in the 2016 Presidential Election." *Journal of Politics* 81(1):296–302.

Larson, Stephanie G. 2006. *Media & minorities: The Politics of race in news and entertainment.* Rowan & Littlefield.

Lewandowsky, Stephan, Ullrich K. H. Ecker and John Cook. 2017. "Beyond misinformation: Understanding and coping with the "post-truth" era." *Journal of Applied Research in Memory and Cognition* 6(4):353–369. **URL:** *www.sciencedirect.com/science/article/pii/S2211368117300700*

Lipsitz, George. 1998. *The possessive investment in whiteness: How white people profit from identity politics.* Temple University Press.

Lopez, Ian Haney. 1997. *White by law: The legal construction of race.* NYU Press.

Lopez, Jesse and D. Sunshine Hillygus. 2018. "Why so serious?: Survey trolls and misinformation." SSRN.
URL: *https://papers.ssrn.com/sol3/papers.cfm?abstract_id=3131087*

Lupia, Arthur. 2016. *Uninformed: Why people know so little about politics and what we can do about it.* Oxford University Press.

Martin, Gregory J. and Ali Yurukoglu. 2017. "Bias in cable news: Persuasion and polarization." *American Economic Review* 107(9):2565–2599.

Mason, Lilliana. 2018. "Ideologues without issues: The polarizing consequences of ideological identities." *Public Opinion Quarterly* 82(S1): 866–887.

McConahay, J. B. 1986. "Modern racism, ambivalence, and the Modern Racism Scale." *Modern racism, ambivalence, and the Modern Racism Scale,* 40(J. F. Dovidio & S. L. Gaertner (eds.)):91–125.

Mendelberg, Tali. 2001. *The race card: Campaign strategy, implicit messages, and the norm of equality.* Princeton University Press.

Michener, Jamila. 2019. "Policy feedback in a racialized polity." *Policy Studies Journal* 47(2):423–450.

Miller, Joanne M., Kyle L. Saunders and Christina E. Farhart. 2016. "Conspiracy endorsement as motivated reasoning: The moderating roles of political knowledge and trust." *American Journal of Political Science* 60(4):824–844.
URL: *https://onlinelibrary.wiley.com/doi/abs/10.1111/ajps.12234*

Min, Seong-Jae and John C. Feaster. 2010. "Missing children in national news coverage: Racial and gender representations of missing children cases." *Communication Research Reports* 27(3):207–216.
URL: *https://doi.org/10.1080/08824091003776289*

Mitchell, Joshua L. and Brendan Toner. 2016. "Exploring the foundations of US state-level anti-sharia initiatives." *Politics and Religion* 9(4):720–743.

Moses, Michele S., Daryl J. Maeda and Christina H. Paguyo. 2019. "Racial politics, resentment, and affirmative action: Asian Americans as 'model' college applicants." *The Journal of Higher Education* 90(1):1–26.

Mutz, Diana C. 2002. "Cross-cutting social networks: Testing democratic theory in practice." *American Political Science Review* 96(1):111–126.

Nacos, Brigette and Oscar Torres-Reyna. 2007. *Fueling our fears: Stereotyping, media coverage, and public opinion of Muslim Americans.* Rowman and Littlefield.

Ngai, Mae M. 2014. *Impossible subjects: Illegal aliens and the making of modern America.* Updated ed. Vol. 105. Princeton University Press.

Nithyanand, Rishab, Brian Schaffner and Phillipa Gill. 2017. "Online political discourse in the Trump era." *arXiv preprint arXiv:1711.05303.*

Nyhan, Brendan. 2010. Why the "death panel" myth wouldn't die: Misinformation in the health care reform debate. In *The Forum.* Vol. 8. De Gruyter.

Nyhan, Brendan and Jason Reifler. 2010. "When corrections fail: The persistence of political misperceptions." *Political Behavior* 32(2):303–330.

Nyhan, Brendan and Jason Reifler. 2015. "Estimating fact-checking's effects." *Arlington, VA: American Press Institute.*

Nyhan, Brendan, Jason Reifler and Peter A. Ubel. 2013. "The hazards of correcting myths about health care reform." *Medical Care* pp. 127–132.

Ojeda, Christopher, Anne M Whitesell, Michael B Berkman and Eric Plutzer. 2019. "Federalism and the Racialization of Welfare Policy." *State Politics & Policy Quarterly* 19(4):474–501.

Orfield, Gary and John T. Yunn. 1999. "Resegregation in American schools.". **URL:** *https://civilrightsproject.ucla.edu/research/k-12-education/integration-and-diversity/resegregation-in-american-schools/orfiled-resegregation-in-american-schools-1999.pdf*

Oskooii, Kassra A. R, Karam Dana and Matthew A. Barreto. 2019. "Beyond generalized ethnocentrism: Islam-specific beliefs and prejudice toward Muslim Americans." *Politics, Groups, and Identities* pp. 1–28.

Oskooii, Kassra A. R., Nazita Lajevardi and Loren Collingwood. 2019. "Opinion shift and stability: The information environment and long-lasting opposition to Trump's Muslim ban." *Political Behavior* pp. 1–37.

Parker, Christopher S. 2009. "When politics becomes protest: Black veterans and political activism in the postwar South." *The Journal of Politics* 71(1):113–131.

Pask, Gordon. 1976. *Conversation theory: Applications in education and epistemology.* Elsevier.

Pearson, Adam R., Jonathon P. Schuldt, Rainer Romero-Canyas, Matthew T. Ballew and Dylan Larson-Konar. 2018. "Diverse segments of the US public underestimate the environmental concerns of minority and low-income Americans." *Proceedings of the National Academy of Sciences* 115(49):12429–12434.

Peffley, Mark and Jon Hurwitz. 2002. "The racial components of "race-neutral" crime policy attitudes." *Political Psychology* 23(1):59–75.

Peffley, Mark, Jon Hurwitz and Jeffery Mondak. 2017. "Racial attributions in the justice system and support for punitive crime policies." *American Politics Research* 45(6):1032–1058.

Pérez, Efren. 2016. *Unspoken politics: Implicit attitudes and political thinking.* Cambridge University Press.

Pérez, Efrén O. 2015. "Xenophobic rhetoric and its political effects on immigrants and their co-ethnics." *American Journal of Political Science* 59(3):549–564.

Pettigrew, Thomas F. 1997. "Generalized intergroup contact effects on prejudice." *Personality and Social Psychology Bulletin* pp. 173–185.

Popkin, Samuel L. 1994. *The reasoning voter: Communication and persuasion in presidential campaigns.* University of Chicago Press.

Reardon, Sean F., Lindsay Fox and Joseph Townsend. 2015. "Neighborhood income composition by household race and income, 1990–2009." *The ANNALS of the American Academy of Political and Social Science* 660(1):78–97.

　　URL: *https://doi.org/10.1177/0002716215576104*

Redlawsk, David P. 2002. "Hot cognition or cool consideration? Testing the effects of motivated reasoning on political decision making." *Journal of Politics* 64(4):1021–1044.

　　URL: *https://onlinelibrary.wiley.com/doi/abs/10.1111/1468-2508.00161*

Rippy, Alyssa E. and Elana Newman. 2006. "Perceived religious discrimination and its relationship to anxiety and paranoia among Muslim Americans." *Journal of Muslim Mental Health* 1(1):5–20.

Said, Edward. 1978 *Orientalism.* New York: Vintage

Salinas, Eduardo. 2020. "Affirmative action for whom? An experiment on Latino policy preferences."

　　URL: *https://preprints.apsanet.org/engage/apsa/article-details/5ec52d804 4d2c2001968b9cc*

Santa Ana, Otto. 2002. *Brown tide rising: Metaphors of Latinos in contemporary American public discourse.* University of Texas Press.

Schaffner, Brian F. and Cameron Roche. 2016. "Misinformation and motivated reasoning: Responses to economic news in a politicized environment." *Public Opinion Quarterly* 81(1):86–110.

Schaffner, Brian F. and Samantha Luks. 2018. "Misinformation or expressive responding? What an inauguration crowd can tell us about the source of political misinformation in surveys." *Public Opinion Quarterly* 82(1):135–147.

　　URL: *https://doi.org/10.1093/poq/nfx042*

Scheufele, Dietram A. and Nicole M. Krause. 2019. "Science audiences, misinformation, and fake news." *Proceedings of the National Academy of Sciences* 116(16):7662–7669.

　　URL: *www.pnas.org/content/116/16/7662*

Schumpeter, Joseph Alois. 1950. *Capitalism, Socialism, and Democracy.* Harper and Brothers.

Sediqe, Nura A. 2020. "Stigma consciousness and American identity: The case of Muslims in the United States." *PS: Political Science & Politics* pp. 1–5.

Segura, Gary M and Ali A Valenzuela. 2010. "Hope, tropes, and dopes: Hispanic and white racial animus in the 2008 election." *Presidential Studies Quarterly* 40(3):497–514.

Selod, Saher. 2015. "Citizenship denied: The racialization of Muslim American men and women post-9/11." *Critical Sociology* 41(1):77–95.

Shaheen, Jack G. 2003. "Reel bad Arabs: How Hollywood vilifies a people." *The Annals of the American Academy of Political and Social Science* 588(1):171–193.

Shaheen, Jack G. 2007. "Hollywood's Muslim Arabs." *Muslim World* 90(1):22–42.

Sides, John and Kimberly Gross. 2013. "Stereotypes of Muslims and support for the war on terror." *The Journal of Politics* 75(3):583–598.

Smith, Candis Watts. 2014. *Black mosaic: The politics of Black pan-ethnic diversity*. New York University Press.

Smith, Rogers M. 1997. *Civic ideals: Conflicting visions of citizenship in US history*. Yale University Press.

Smith, Rogers M. 2003. *Stories of peoplehood: The politics and morals of political membership*. Cambridge University Press.

Sunstein, Cass R. 2018. *# Republic: Divided democracy in the age of social media*. Princeton University Press.

Swami, Viren. 2012. "Social psychological origins of conspiracy theories: The case of the Jewish conspiracy theory in Malaysia." *Frontiers in Psychology* 3:280.
  URL: *www.frontiersin.org/article/10.3389/fpsyg.2012.00280*

Taber, Charles S. and Milton Lodge. 2006. "Motivated skepticism in the evaluation of political beliefs." *American Journal of Political Science* 50(3):755–769.
  URL: *https://onlinelibrary.wiley.com/doi/abs/10.1111/j.1540-5907.2006.00 214.x*

Tate, Katherine. 1994. *From protest to politics: The new black voters in American elections*. Harvard University Press.

Taylor, Robert Joseph, Reuben Miller, Dawne Mouzon, Verna M. Keith and Linda M. Chatters. 2018. "Everyday discrimination among African American men: The impact of criminal justice contact." *Race and justice* 8(2):154–177.

Tesler, Michael. 2012. "The spillover of racialization into health care: How President Obama polarized public opinion by racial attitudes and race." *American Journal of Political Science* 56(3):690–704.
  URL: *https://onlinelibrary.wiley.com/doi/abs/10.1111/j.1540-5907.2011.00 577.x*

Tesler, Michael. 2016. *Post-racial or most-racial?: Race and politics in the Obama Era*. University of Chicago Press.

Tesler, Michael and David Sears. 2010. *Obama's Race: The 2008 election and the dream of a post-racial America.* University of Chicago Press.

Thomas, Susan L. 1998. "Race, gender, and welfare reform: The antinatalist response." *Journal of Black Studies* 28(4):419–446.

Thornbury, Scott and Diana Slade. 2006. *Conversation: From description to pedagogy.* Cambridge University Press.

Thorson, Emily. 2016. "Belief echoes: The persistent effects of corrected misinformation." *Political Communication* 33(3):460–480.
URL: *https://doi.org/10.1080/10584609.2015.1102187*

Tyree, Tia. 2011. "African American stereotypes in reality television." *Howard Journal of Communications* 22(4):394–413.

Valentino, Nicholas A., Ted Brader and Ashley E. Jardina. 2013*a*. "Immigration opposition among U.S. Whites: General ethnocentrism or media priming of attitudes about Latinos?" *Political Psychology* 34(2):149–166.
URL: *https://onlinelibrary.wiley.com/doi/abs/10.1111/j.1467-9221.2012.00 928.x*

Valentino, Nicholas A., Ted Brader and Ashley E. Jardina. 2013*b*. "Immigration opposition among US Whites: General ethnocentrism or media priming of attitudes about Latinos?" *Political Psychology* 34(2):149–166.

Walker, Hannah, Marcel Roman and Matt Barreto. 2020. "The ripple effect: The political consequences of proximal contact with immigration enforcement." *Journal of Race, Ethnicity and Politics* 5(3):537–572.

Wallace, Sophia Jordán and Chris Zepeda-Millán. 2020. *Walls, cages, and family separation: Race and immigration policy in the Trump era.* Cambridge University Press.

Waters, Mary C., Philip Kasinitz and Asad L. Asad. 2014. "Immigrants and African Americans." *Annual Review of Sociology* 40:369–390.

Weaver, Vesla M. and Amy E. Lerman. 2010. "Political consequences of the carceral state." *American Political Science Review* pp. 817–833.

Wetts, Rachel and Robb Willer. 2018. "Privilege on the precipice: Perceived racial status threats lead White Americans to oppose welfare programs." *Social Forces* 97(2):793–822.

Williamson, Scott. 2019. "Countering misperceptions to reduce prejudice: An experiment on attitudes toward Muslim Americans." *Journal of Experimental Political Science* pp. 1–12.

Wilson, David C., Michael Leo Owens and Darren W. Davis. 2015. "How racial attitudes and ideology affect political rights for felons." *Du Bois Review* 12(1):73.

Wood, Thomas and Ethan Porter. 2019. "The elusive backfire effect: Mass attitudes' steadfast factual adherence." *Political Behavior* 41(1):135–163.

Yazdiha, Haj. 2014. "Law as movement strategy: How the Islamophobia movement institutionalizes fear through legislation." *Social Movement Studies* 13(2):267–274.

Young, Iris Marion. 1990. *Justice and the politics of difference*. Princeton University Press.

Cambridge Elements

Race, Ethnicity, and Politics

Megan Ming Francis
University of Washington

Megan Ming Francis is Associate Professor of Political Science at the University of Washington and Fellow at the Ash Center for Democratic Governance and the Carr Center for Human Rights at the Harvard Kennedy School. Francis is the author of the award winning book, *Civil Rights and the Making of the Modern American State*. She is particularly interested in American political and constitutional development, social movements, the criminal punishment system, Black politics, philanthropy, and the post–Civil War South.

About the Series

Elements in Race, Ethnicity, and Politics is an innovative publishing initiative in the social sciences. The series publishes important original research that breaks new ground in the study of race, ethnicity, and politics. It welcomes research that speaks to the current political moment, research that provides new perspectives on established debates, and interdisciplinary research that sheds new light on previously understudied topics and groups.

Cambridge Elements $\equiv$

Race, Ethnicity, and Politics

Elements in the Series

Walls, Cages, and Family Separation: Race and Immigration Policy in the Trump Era
Sophia Jordán Wallace, Chris Zepeda-Millán

(Mis)Informed: What Americans Know About Social Groups and Why it Matters for Politics
Marisa Abrajano, Nazita Lajevardi

A full series listing is available at: www.cambridge.org/EREP

Printed in the United States
by Baker & Taylor Publisher Services